How to Plan a Great Second Life

Why not live fully every day
of your extra 30 years?

Gordon Burgett

Communication Unlimited
Santa Maria, California

ISBN 0-9708621-4-8

Disclaimer: This book is designed to provide information in regard to the subject matter covered. It is sold with the understanding that the publisher and author are not engaged in rendering legal, medical, financial, or other professional services. If such expert assistance is desired or required, the services of a competent professional should be sought.

Published by Communication Unlimited, P.O. Box 6405, Santa Maria, CA 93456 / (800) 563-1454 / fax (805) 937-3035. Other fine Communication Unlimited publications are available from your bookstore or directly from the publisher. See related information at the end of this book or check http://www.super-second-life.com.

Acknowledgements

The world is full of productive, vibrant Second Lifers. I've been fortunate to have among my friends many models of how a second life should be lived, though they will shudder to see their names in print for doing nothing more than being vital, good, loving people. I'm thinking of Lu Hintz, whose days are spent trying to birdie the sixteenth hole while at night he sings in quartets, creates a newsletter, and teaches English to immigrants—and of his wife, Mary, who is even busier! Of Larry Los, who delivers Meals on Wheels, is active in a half-dozen other groups, travels, and also sings with the local barbershoppers. I'm thinking of my N.S.A. Gold Coast comrades, my twin brother Bill and his wife Judy, many fellow warblers, and a dozen others who have come into their own as they age and are making the world better because of their wisdom, compassion, and efficacy. They don't need my book. They're just figuring it out themselves.

Conversely, my heart goes out to those who seem to unplug at about 55 or 60. I feel helpless in their presence. That's one reason I'm updating this book. It's a way I know to help them—and myself, who is suddenly their age and never thought much about either a first or second life, until the first was almost over and the second arrived, unbeckoned.

This second edition gives me a chance to showcase two gifted kin. Doug Burgett, my nephew, designed the covers. It is the second time I've been lucky enough to use his skills. And my sister, Nancy Burgett, proofed these pages. If errors or inanity still survived and reached print, it's despite her best efforts!

Contents

Introduction

PART ONE.   Getting Ready for a Great Second Life

PART TWO.   Planning, Implementing, and Living
a Great Second Life

Appendix

Lists, Forms, and Worksheets

Introduction

An absurd idea...

When I was ten, a book like this would have seemed absurd. That was 1948 and mostly I remember two things—a loud neighborhood party when the war ended (that was World War II, and we were supposedly sound asleep several doors away) and my mother crying when Franklin Delano Roosevelt died.

During my earlier years, say 20 to 40, I was too busy just surviving and doing what everybody else did to give it much thought. My only sense of mortality was one night, at 38, realizing that I would no longer get that desperate call from the Cubs to put on the gear, get behind the plate, and bring them a pennant. Old age and death seemed a million years away.

The crack in my immortality came when I was 50, the year my 27-year marriage hit the shoals while our girls were in Europe celebrating the near-miraculous bestowal of their college degrees. Suddenly the future seemed endless. I'd never thought about retirement, hobbies, or later-life goals. The infinite was finite. If I could work forever, I could live forever. I needed this book then, but it didn't exist.

Blame the "Boomers"!

That it does exist you can blame on the "boomers"—if you're into blaming. It took their reaching 50 to provide much public focus on a sensible, rewarding older age.

What put my pen in this pasture was a chance remark on the radio, something about our current life expectancy being about 80 and the 50-80 later-life vacuum being just as long as the maturing bubble for those 20-50.

Then just about everything I heard or read for the next two weeks seemed to be about retirement and nobody being prepared—like me. Was that true? I love research, I'm a writer, and the line was drawn.

This book has answers

What I found is on these pages.

I was sixty when I started this book. I'm 65 now and the first printing has sold out. In the past five years I also offered scores of speeches and workshops about second life planning and design. To my delight, I found that my book was on track and its contents were both helpful and need-meeting. So in this second edition I am mildly updating the first, somewhat simplifying the process, making the examples easier to relate to, and releasing it in a smaller paperback form. It even has a new website section accessible at no charge to those who wish to download and print out clean, unused charts and fill-in forms.

I also discovered that hardly a sexagenarian had heard much about or seriously planned for his or her own "second life." But they—we—weren't alone. Those noisy, puffing boomers, bless them, hadn't either. As for anyone younger than them thinking about their later years, I might as well be writing about corset hooks or one-horse shays. (Their day will come...)

A last thought. I could have moaned for several hundred pages about our collective lack of preparation, or just listed 700 or 7,000 ways to get ready. But who wants to read that? What I really want to know (and share with you) is summed up in two questions:

(1) How can you and I lead more joyous and productive years by creating our own "Great Second Life"?

(2) And, specifically, what can we do now to prepare ourselves to live each of the days we have left to its fullest?

The answers are found in Parts One and Two.

This book is a reference guide, a blueprint, and a map all in one. Please take its words and its process and from them create your own wildly exciting, unique, envious Great Second Life.

Enough babbling. Neither of us is getting any younger. Let me find my specs and let's get going...

"Life without love is a bird without a song. Life without trust is a night without day. Life without faith is a tree without root. Life without hope is a year without Spring. Life without friends is a sun without shade. Life without work is a bloom without fruit."

Dr. William Arthur Ward

Part One

Getting Ready for a Great Second Life

"The advantage of being eighty years old is that one has had many people to love."

Jean Renoir

Chapter 1

What Are You Going to Do With Your Extra 30 Years?

So you're 40 or 50, big deal. The only question that counts is "What are you going to do with your next 30 years?"

Nobody in the history of man has lived as long as you—and ended up in such good shape.

Your ancestors had kids, but rarely saw their kids have kids. Most women never knew menopause. Men died when their legs, eyes, or ears failed.

In 1900, the average life expectancy was 48. Now it's 78, scarcely a hundred years later. For most, 30 extra years! What a wonderful problem!

So here you are, feeling fine, looking good, full of ginger, all gussied up and historically with no place to go.

You might as well make a plan that will use all your knowledge and experience, your values and laughter, in those "new" 30 years.

Your parents, certainly theirs, subscribed to the "declining philosophy" that said that from midlife on it was all downhill, that the party was over, dreams unrealized were just that. But today that's as out of date as your prom dress, ball glove, or 8-tracks. People now don't just curl up and die when they hit the 50-yard line. In fact, most bloom like never before. Better yet, they have the skill, strength, wisdom, and experience—sometimes even the money—to make their second half the joyous completion of what the first half prepared them to do.

Of course, whether that happens to you is pretty much your choice. Just sitting around waiting to die can take a long time, if curling up is your thing...

You at least deserve some options to use between then and now. Plenty of books tell you to save billions for your "retirement." Others urge you to volunteer 26 hours a day. But none shows you how to take your future by the reins and make it go precisely where you wish.

This book has that goal: to help you plan the rest of your days.

You can use it to map out the great unknown—your Great Second Life!

Then you will have a hundred options, a hundred alternatives, and maybe a hundred new friends.

What the book is all about

Extra years...

Of all the people who *ever* reached 65 years of age, one half of them are alive today!

If you lived to half that age during the Dark Ages, you were very, very old. Living too many years has hardly been a historical problem!

The miracle is that most of us will live into our 80s, and some far beyond 100. We may even know a person who will live to 200.

How valuable are those extra years? They're only worth having if they are worth living.

No strings attached

We get 30 more years just for being alive shortly after the end of a century rather than at its start—a gift with no strings attached!

That's how much life expectancy has increased since 1900. Years to do with as we wish. We *all* get them, or at least the chance at them.

But who reading these pages has a plan for them? We didn't plan our first life, and when we hit the 40s and early 50s, when the gift kicks in, we have no plan for the extra years either.

I'm not scolding. I'm 65 and never gave a thought to any of this: extra years, a plan, a gift-horse, until I learned about that life expectancy in 1900 and realized that my grandmothers lived to about 90, and it hit me that I'm spending my gift without even knowing that I'd gotten it. Just frittering it away, for the most part.

Yet if you and I had a plan we could take this gift, this jewel, and cut it and set it ourselves and make it shine. If we considered these extra 30 years our second life, our gift life, we could finally do what we wanted to do by intent, free from the toil and expectations and often the sheer nonsense of our first life.

Thirty free years. A gift horse. With a plan, that's found gold.

All we need is an Action Plan

So let me help you, and me, do that. Let's start creating Action Plans for our own Great Second Lives.

This book, then, is not about "retirement." Most of us reading it will not retire in the way our parents did (and the way the government wanted, so we would open up jobs for the young). We won't be throwing down our hod or rug beaters at 65, bent and shot.

When the "Iron Chancellor" Otto von Bismarck, in the late 1800s, plucked a retirement age of 70 out of the air, thinking it so old that the German state would hardly have to pay pensions at all, it was far beyond the average life expectancy.

When F.D.R. created an old-age retirement system in the United States, and lowered it to 65, it still was. Today, a person 65 will probably be line dancing two decades later.

Nor is this book solely directed to the 40 plus. In truth, it should be mandatory reading in high school, or college at the latest, so the readers could plan both their first *and* second lives—and make each far better.

But that will never happen. Kids in their late teens and 20s are too juicy and jumpy, invincible, and all-knowing. They might agree that there's a kernel of truth to what these pages say but they'd consider it about as applicable as a Byzantine grunt.

The best time to start planning?

This is a book designed to help you use your gift to its fullest by creating your own Great Second Life. That's when the very best living takes place, or can. But for that to be so requires thought, some planning, decisions made, and some dreams dreamed and action acted.

So I chose 40 as an arbitrary time to start planning and suspect that most of the readers will tune in between then and 55, an age when thinking about going backwards to become a kid again makes your fewer hairs stand straight up in horror. You've outgrown that posturing and madness. Anyway, nature won't let you.

The problem is what you think you see ahead: less power, less beauty, less passion, less money, and less years.

You need better eyes. The truth is, the second half of your life will be better, more exciting, and much more in your control than the hard half you're escaping.

You're in midlife, and as soon as you stop yelling "Crisis!" and waltz through it, you're going to pop out a new, calmer, stronger person.

And since you had the wisdom to buy a book telling you how to create a "Great Second Life," not only are you going to be ready to leap into your new body and mind to enjoy your second journey, you're also going to be able to extract every last drop of joy from it.

Part Two of this book

In the second half of this book I'll walk you, step-by-step, through a straightforward process of planning, then implementing, for those years. It starts with a Dream List and ends with a detailed Action Plan for the coming stages of your life. (If your dream machine has gotten rusty, I'll even share 200 rather generic dreams in the Appendix from which you might choose.)

But in this half let's talk about that dreaded "midlife crisis," nature, liberation, what you did right, and what you want to shuck as soon as you can. Then we'll discuss the business of staying healthy and a different look at staying solvent, before we figure out how to spend that vigor and cash!

Why plan at all? Why not just let it happen?

The best answer may be that since you didn't plan for the first half and you've only got the second half left, do you want to be planless your entire life?

I know, you did plan the first half—without my book.

Malarkey. You've been led around by the hormones for most of the last 40 years, and when they didn't drag you from school to marriage to babies (all in the name of sex, and maybe love), then society kicked in and picked the order and the rituals while delineating the restraints. Don't fret: nature and society enslaved us all, and it wasn't so bad. We've paid our reproductive dues, have kids we love, and despite ourselves half the time, built up a kitbag of knowledge and skills. We even pocketed some coins and slipped in some fun.

Sure, you chose your spouse, picked your job, and have been in control of every facet of your life from the time you were six. Yep, and there's a gold bar glued to the back of this book.

See Chapter 4 for more about those early years and what we will gladly leave behind.

The point is: whatever the past, you survived it and came out ahead.

Now you've got 30 more years and this time you *are* in charge. So why not take all those street smarts, school learning, and people skills and put them to full use to design the kind of life you want, then make that happen?

The last days of your only life

In Chapter 8 you will be asked a simple question: "If you had all the money, time, and energy you needed and were free from any outside constraints, what would you do in your extra 30 years?" From the answers, you create your own Dream List. What's left is the defining and doing.

It's your life and your last days. You get one life and a lot of last days. Why not look through new eyes and plan a new path, which likely includes much of the old path but cleaned up, straightened, and with a higher purpose? Why not make certain that what's important, or exciting, or flat-out incredible is *yours*—by intent, not happenchance?

The alternative isn't dreadful. It's just more todays forever. It's what 99.98% of all people have done since the discovery of fire and ashtrays. And what almost all of your friends will do (unless you're kind enough to share this book with them).

But why would *you* leave something as important as 30 years of your only life to fate, chance, or fortune? Or, worse yet, your memory!

Why wouldn't you congratulate yourself for all of the good things you've done, take a long look at what you've yet to do, dip into your dream bag to see what more you could add to the roster, factor in your health and coffers, touch base with your mate, then put all that down on paper, creating a clear map of where you intend to go to finish the journey that was earlier interrupted (by sex, confusion, frustration, mayhem, at least one incredibly daft boss, and bad music) but is now open to completion?

Before we delve into planning, let's address two related concerns, in reverse order of importance. The first asks, "If this planning a Great Second Life is such a hot idea, why didn't my folks do it?" Of all the dumb stuff they did do, they never mentioned it.

The second is more important. It simply says that it doesn't matter what we plan, we're going to lose or forget about the plans, give up on them, or just laugh at the exercise a few months after it's finished. Heavens. More on that in a moment.

So, why weren't our folks as wise as we are when it comes to creating a specific plan for the second half of our lives? Four reasons come quickly to mind:

1. Their expectations came directly from what they'd seen their parents do. In our grandparents' time, few lived beyond 60 and they were patterned into a life of working until retirement, then hanging on until death.
2. Our grandparents probably lived at home (or within a mile) and in effect were dependents again, so there was no reason to plan. They usually had chores to perform and were a vital part of the household.
3. Even if they wanted to work longer or lead more active lives, the number of available service jobs were extremely limited, travel was much harder, and as long as they lived at or near home and spent within their pension or Social Security allotments, there was little incentive to do more.
4. And they were just plumb tired. Labor then meant manual, at work or at home, and jobs demanded plenty of it. The key

part of "retirement" was "tire." Add a "d" and any stimulus to a vital, active post-work life was gone. Medicines and treatment were still relatively primitive, nutrition was substandard, and one's stamina at 55 was like a 75 year-old's today.

We're on our own!

Today, our lives now are markedly different. At 55, we still have those extra 30 years to live. Even if our kids did expect us to return home, there's no room. Instead, they more likely expect us to be independent as long as we can, then slip into some sort of aided-living home before we die in a hospital. They would be grateful if we did this without interrupting their schedules; doubly grateful if we simply told them what we had done after the fact. Except death. If we die without pre-warning them, they'll never forgive us. A few day's warning is perfect.

They presume we will patch together the government support—Social Security and Medicare—and add our pension, insurance, and savings to it to have enough money to take care of all future needs, including medical and burial. If we don't do this, we are irresponsible. (They wouldn't refuse a small inheritance either.)

Not that we'll be completely detached. The telephone can keep us in touch if we have emergency needs. And we aren't nearly as isolated as our grandparents were, with radio (we still listen to radios), television, computers, and sometimes accessible public transport (after driving becomes difficult).

As long as we don't mortify our kids (tiptoeing, out of sight, is best), we can even do "young" things and no one seems to care.

In fact, we're not as old as our counterparts decades back. We eat better, do less physically taxing work, keep working more years, pay more attention to our health, have more information at our disposal about maintaining a healthy life, exercise, have more seniors to mix with, are far more open about mental health, and have a stronger web of services we can draw upon.

So why shouldn't we plan our own best lives for the second half? Society is indifferent (though it will try to sell us anything it thinks we're addled enough to buy). Our kids are permissive; turnabout is indeed fair play. It's our money, what there is of it, and our time, which is more abundant. And, to repeat, "here we are, feeling fine, looking good, full of ginger, all gussied up and historically with no place to go." May as well mortify the kids and do what we want when we want. The meter's ticking. If we plan it right, we can be a constant 30-year mortification machine.

We've still got plenty of marbles!

The supposition that whether we plan a "Great Second Life" or not, we'll be incapable of carrying out the plans or will lose interest sounds suspiciously like saying that we begin the mental and attitudinal slippery slide sometime in the 50s (or sooner), and it gets progressively faster and steeper until we're lucky to find our shoes, much less tie them, when we reach antiquity. (Go Velcro!)

Sometimes that is true, and then it's not at all funny. There are mental disorders, but they hold steady at about 5% of the populace at every age. Seniors have no edge there. And there are forms of latter-life dementia and illnesses, including, of course, Alzheimer's. They are tragedies for all involved.

But most folks don't change much during their later years, beyond the usual physical aging and decline in short-term memory. The fear of mental incompetence is for most groundless. The danger is that we will accept the false assumption that all mental functions decline with age, then act out the stereotype, withdrawing and losing self-esteem and becoming a self-fulfilling prophecy.

Intelligence tests show little change as one ages, although one gets slower (and more cautious). We do process sensory information slower and take longer to perceive a stimulus, and slower yet when the task is complicated or a surprise. "We continue to gain rather than decline in our ability to manage our daily affairs; it is usually only in times of stress or loss that our mechanisms may be pushed beyond their limits," says Dr. Mark E. Williams in *The Complete Guide to Aging and Health*.

Even better, our response to physical stimulus needn't change at all—and will actually be faster if we take part in regular physical activity.

Three second life components deserve comment: learning, satisfaction with life, and personal control.

Learning

Our capacity to learn continues throughout life. That capacity is divided into three phases of information processing: encoding, storage, and retrieval.

Encoding is mentally registering information. We get worse at it as we age, but that may be linked to hearing or vision—barriers to having the information understood. We are best when we can link visual information to its audio component.

Our recall ability, to search and retrieve information from storage, worsens over time, but there is little decline in our ability to match our information in storage with information in the environment.

While our short-term memory is the biggest change with aging (what did I say?), our long-term memory declines only a bit, and that is probably due to poorer encoding. Very long-term memory gets better from 20-50 and holds steady until about 70. Maybe it is overwhelmed after 70 because we've gathered up so much to remember!

Mostly we compensate and get along fine (as long as we pin our keys to our sleeve and write where we're going on our hand). What throws us off is a new challenge, like new surroundings, or major stress, like the loss of a spouse.

Satisfaction and control

One imagines that the older we get, the less satisfied with life we become. Except for the extremely old, life satisfaction doesn't decrease with age, despite all the factors that could influence it, like poorer health, loss of a spouse or friends, and less money or activity. People simply adapt to those situations that can't be changed. And elders report less stress: they cope better and expect less.

A lot of it has to do with attitude. "The attitude we take about aging will be very important in affecting the success with which we age," says Dr. Williams. "Meaningful participation in family and community activities is a major source of personal satisfaction and is the product of cultural attitudes and decisions made earlier in life."

A plan for a purposeful second life could play a key role in that later level of personal satisfaction.

A sense of personal control is critical to our overall well-being. Personal control is the ability to manipulate aspects of our environment, and the inability to do that results in feelings of helplessness and depression. A loss of perceived control can happen to older folk, particularly when they have a disability. It can produce adverse affects (rage, depression, violence, abuse), even death. They simply give up.

Which is, again, where a plan for life built of choices is useful. Even if all of the plans fail to materialize, just the ability to predict events may be a form of control in that it allows us to adapt to the situation.

Dr. Williams adds,

The acceptance of limits and a finite future is a quality of maturity, not a matter of resignation or defeat. With years of rich experience and reflection, some of us can transcend our own circumstances. We call this ability to see the truth in the light of the moment, wisdom. So as we age in creativity, in deepening wisdom and sensibility we become *more*, not less. And we realize that aging confronts us with the tension between ourselves now and ourselves in the future. We have an enormous amount of choice regarding our own aging. What are we sowing, and what is it we wish to reap?"

More about our physical and mental health in Chapter 6.

Planning and choice, then, is what this book is about. Plan and choose how you will best use this 30-year gift; how you will keep your body and mind tuned and in control of a life loved and fully lived.

Chapter 2

What Base Did You Build During Those First 40+ Years?

We're all nature's slaves until we're useless to the breeding imperative, and most of what we did—particularly from about 12 through the 20s (and even 30s)—was basically out of our control.

Nonetheless, you got taught, learned skills, found values, developed a personality, and discovered areas of strength and passion that you want to be part of your life forever.

Whatever the cause, you came to love tennis, teaching, baking, or painting on wood. A future life without work, reading, golf, playing with the grandtykes, or doodling in web graphics would be unthinkable.

And you gathered up achievements in specific disciplines or directions while you grew up. Along the way you found things you wanted to explore in depth or experience first-hand when you no longer needed the job income, when time was your own.

So here you start recording those strengths, passions, and directions that you want to carry over into your second life, to become a part, even the core, of your later life Action Plan. And what you want to leave properly behind.

You identify the things you particularly value today to include in your coming second life

We are busy, walking wonders

If we ever began with a *tabula rasa*—that famous blank slate upon which our history is written—it is brim full by the time we're 40 or 50, with squiggly notes on the sides and a couple of Post-Its wagging off the edge.

We've managed to cram in more living in the first half of our lives than we imagine or give ourselves credit for.

The bigger achievements we acknowledge and detail on our résumés and curriculum vitae: schools attended, degrees or certificates attained, jobs or positions held, and awards received.

And we're certain to recall the people we married, children brought into the world, places lived, and hobbies or special events enjoyed.

But there's a lot of other things we take for granted that would seem extraordinary if seen from peasant's eyes centuries back. They have given us a depth unimagined by even the most visionary not that long ago.

Think of all we have done...

We have probably visited a half-dozen foreign countries, yet even if we've never left our state, through television, movies, and videos we can draw real sweat from vicariously paddling through a steamy forest in New Guinea or gasping for oxygen climbing those last 200 yards up the snowy, swirling Mount Everest.

Without even knowing how it's done, we can e-mail to Bali, find an exotic recipe for *feijoada baiana*, or bid on a newly found Grecian vase.

We drive cars more powerful and dangerous than a herd of buffalo, read whole books, write whole letters, hear music performed by symphony orchestras half a globe away, understand depression, successfully interact with more people in one day than our ancestors saw in a lifetime, and live whole lives without need of a weapon.

We are, flat-out, walking wonders, with a brain that would be the marvel of any world. In our own, we are top dogs; animals know things, but we know that we know things. We balance jobs, families, necessities, fun, and charity, with time left over to flirt, read to our kids, whistle, daydream, and shingle a shed.

So what we've done in our first 40 or 50 years would astound our grandparents and be utterly unbelievable to their grandparents.

What's Next?

Whew! That was just the first half. We've still got 30 years left—a whole second life, into which we bring knowledge, polished skills, friends, professional contacts, maturity, social stability, enough street savvy to at least not lose what we possess, enough humor to stay sane and do our business, and enough vigor and cunning to pick out which cards we need to play a winning hand.

After all, our first life doesn't just end and all that we gathered disappear.

In fact, we must create an awareness of having two lives, which is a secondary purpose of this book. We must, at some point, realize that much of what worked in our early years was needed then but is inappropriate, if not counterproductive, later. At the gateway between those lives we must become the gatekeeper, to take stock and let pass most of the skills and knowledge, stop many of the behaviors and attitudes that were nature-driven but are useless after fertility becomes impossible or irrelevant, and question much of the rest. More on those behaviors in Chapter 4.

The problem is determining what we want to let into our second lives.

Some defining tools should help

The second half of this book will indeed help us define what we want to do during those latter years, and, by extension, what is needed to make that happen.

If we've been hapless scoundrels the first half, there's much to be left behind plus a new attitude and supportive skills to obtain for life number two. If we led a driven, job-intensive life but now want to pursue a second career interspersed with much travel and filmmaking, we're on the path to making that happen.

Of course, we will continue to learn, adding new knowledge and skills to our slate in the second half. If it's necessary later, we will acquire what we don't have now, just as we did in our first life.

At this point, a few tools might help us tend that gate. They will also be helpful later when we design our "Great Second Life."

Looking backward to see forward

The most important is a no-nonsense look at what we did in our first life. More than another résumé, it is our own listing of what was important, what we learned from it, what we want to discontinue now, what we want to take with us into our second life, and, after looking at all that, what comes to mind that would add joy and worth to our coming years.

It's your turn! Let's do this by creating five "me now" lists that will help you see more clearly who you are now and who you would like to be in your second life. The lists overlap because some related questions are asked different ways. There is something to be learned from each list, so you'd be best served by doing all five.

But if you don't do any, okay. Or just two or three. Nor is there a grade for excellence, incisiveness, or honesty. The lists can simply help add definition and richness to those coming 30 years.

The first list, appropriately List 1, is the most complex. It asks you to catalogue the most important contributions you have made in your first 40 (or whatever) years, in order of importance. After the contributions, continue to list your achievements, then the activities you performed, also in the order of the satisfaction or pride they brought you. Then, from each item noted, identify the skills developed or strengthened from that contribution, achievement, or activity. Finally, ways you might apply that skill in your second life.

Expand the length of the lists as needed. Remember, the same lists, usually longer, are found in the Appendix.

"ME NOW" LIST 1		
Contributions Achievements Activities	Skills Developed	Ways I might apply these skills in my second life...

If this is a library book, please do not fill in this page! For a free, full-page download of this form, see www.super-second-life.com/form2A.htm

List 1 speaks of skills. List 2 describes you as a person: as you are now and have been, adjectives one might have used to describe you earlier but are no longer applicable, and new adjectives you'd like them to use during your second life.

Why are you doing this? To stop and take stock now, to set up a temporary mental comparison between the way you are now (and were), and to begin to set up some vision (and goals) of how you wish to be (and what you may wish to do) in the future.

"ME NOW" LIST 2		
An objective person would use these adjectives to describe me now	Adjectives no longer applicable that they might have used about me in my first life	New adjectives I would like them to properly use about me during my second life

If this is a library book, please do not fill in this page! For a free, full-page download of this form, see www.super-second-life.com/form2B.htm

The third list asks a similar question but from a broader perspective. First, ten words that would describe your first life. Then, of those ten, which words would you like to continue to describe your second life?

"ME NOW" LIST 3	
These 10 words describe my first life:	I'm putting an "X" by those that I want to continue to describe my second life
1.	
2.	
3.	
4.	
5.	
6.	
7.	
8.	
9.	
10.	

If this is a library book, please do not fill in this page! For a free, full-page download of this form, see www.super-second-life.com/form2C.htm

List 4 is broader yet, and asks for more future projections. It asks what you want to leave at the gate, what you want to carry into your second life, and what additional strengths you wish to develop in your second life.

"ME NOW" LIST 4		
These are attitudes, activities, traits, etc. that I want to leave at the gate	These are strengths I now possess that I want to take into my second life	These are strengths I want to develop in my second life

If this is a library book, please do not fill in this page! For a free, full-page download of this form, see www.super-second-life.com/form2D.htm

Life should be a joy, not just work and worry. The fifth list, a word or two wide, doesn't require retrospection but simply asks you to list ten words that would add *joy* and *worth* to your second life.

"ME NOW" LIST 5	
These 10 words would add joy and worth to my second life	
1.	6.
2.	7.
3.	8.
4.	9.
5.	10.

If this is a library book, please do not fill in this page! For a free, full-page download of this form, see www.super-second-life.com/form2E.htm

What to keep and what to leave

Did you doubt that you had a trove of skills and abilities you were honing during your first life? Look back at your lists, then reflect on how much better prepared you are now to fully live than you were before.

That's what you're bringing into your second life. And what you're leaving behind, as unneeded, undesired, or detrimental to where you want to be this time around.

We don't have a clear view yet of what these next 30 years could be like, but these exercises will help define that plan later.

For now, congratulate yourself on doing them and on caring enough about yourself to have read this far. And give yourself a "good job" on having not only survived this long, but with so much going for you. After all, you're here, intact, and eager to move on. And now you know the secret: the first half is just a loud, sweaty exercise to get you tuned up and mentally ready to live your "Great Second Life!"

How much is your second life worth?

For some, another day or month of life might be worth a fortune. For 30 years, many fortunes!

But for the rest of us, with no fortunes to spare, let's let William Shakespeare suggest a value. He let Richard III set a price when he shouted "A horse! A horse! My kingdom for a horse."

You are the king or queen of your life; it is your kingdom—with your home your castle. So if somebody offered to sell you a whole extra year of life, an entire year in which you could do what you wanted—eliminate poverty, cure cancer, sail, golf or just kick back and read more Shakespeare (or frothy romances)—would that be worth a horse a year?

What's a good horse worth? Maybe $2,000? Plus oats and necessities—maybe another $500? Thus a year might be worth $2,500.

Yet most of us, on the average, get 30 full years. That's 30 times $2,500. Our second life, then, by this odd logic, would be a free gift of $75,000!

If somebody gave me $75,000 with no strings attached but to spend it, I'd sure make a plan before I let the green fly. Which is all this book suggests: you're going to get the gift anyway, so stop now and figure out the best way to use it as fully and with as much joy as possible. Stop horsing around.

Chapter 3

Who Should Plan Your Great Second Life?

Let me ask the question in a different way. "Who should create your second life?"

You.

Not your spouse, your parent(s), your kid(s), the government, your job, or society.

If you've got a mate or dependents, make your own Action Plan, then integrate them into it using the conflict resolution process explained in Chapter 11.

But single, joined, or encumbered, it's your time.

These are the only last years you will ever have. Why waste them? And why try to live somebody else's life at the expense of your own? It's not only impossible, it's a huge waste of your happiness and your potential.

So, you do your own planning. NOW.

Single, mated, or encumbered, you do your own planning—it's your life

---

It's your life

You must create your own second life. Who else? It's *your* life.

The days and what you do with them belong to you—not to your spouse, your parent(s), your kid(s), society, or anyone else.

They are the only days you will ever have. At any age, sitting around waiting for life to lead you somewhere is still just sitting around. You need a plan for what you will do for the rest of your life: *your own plan.*

You're married or have dependents or others you are responsible for? Join the club! Let's address that a bit later in this chapter.

You are important.
You can reshape your next 30 years

The point of these pages is personal responsibility. *You* are important. *You* bring things to this life that no one else can. *You* have a life that counts. *You.*

You can decide to simply live out your days, unplanned, letting circumstances and others direct your fate. (In which case you should stop reading this book; it will frustrate you.)

Or you can be proactive and mold those days as much as you wish or can. You can determine what's important to you and to those you love. You can select what you'd like to learn more about, or see, or experience. You can decide who gets your primary attention, who you want to help, what causes are sufficiently important to deserve your support and promotion, where you want to live, how you can make your life part of a better city, group, or universe—whatever you want!

Is that selfish? Too self-centered? Hardly. If *you* don't take responsibility for yourself and how you will spend your days, then somebody else may have to—and that *is* selfish. They have their own lives to tend to and live.

One alternative, of course, is to take care of others' lives rather than or in addition to your own. Which won't work. You can help others in times of need, but you can no more control their lives than you can direct the wind or manage the stars. And why would you, assuming that your own responsibility is a full-time job?

The ideal is for loving people, all assuming responsibility for their own lives, to then share the extra love that overflows.

What does that mean as it relates to your own second life? It means that you not only think about what you want to do with your extra 30 years, you convert those thoughts into words. Since there is more to doing than simply wishing, it also means that all the variables become part of that plan, including your time, finances, energy, and state of health.

Most of us didn't plan our first life, but we can do better in the second

Most of us did little or no true planning up to this point. Oh sure, we made spot decisions when required, and planned for short trips and how to invest or which car to buy, but full, detailed life plans are about as rare in those under 40 as teeth in worms. Perhaps rightly so: we are under others' control the first half of that time. We live in a trance.

It's curious how we finally get control just about the time that men and women start heading in different directions. For every man who suddenly finds feelings and realizes that winning every race is very, very tiring (if not impossible) there is a woman who suddenly starts itching to get going, in a new-found voice that blows the more timid aside.

If people are going to wake up from their trance and take full reins, it is usually when they are from about 35 to 55, although some do it earlier. That is when we can cut out what isn't working from our youth, build on what is, and focus on solidifying our working and home lives.

This book proposes that we also project from that point until our last days. That each person take responsibility for their entire lives, to maximize the skills and knowledge gathered to create the very best second life possible.

Mates and dependents are people too!

Oh yes, those mates and dependents.

Guess what—they have lives too, however much you suspect they'd like you to plan and lead theirs for them.

So what I'm proposing is no less valid for them to do than it is for you.

There may be exceptions, for you or them. If you are terminally ill and have but a few months left, make a quicker plan, then get living fully now and each remaining day. (Studies show that people who do this are not only happier, they tend to live longer and some heal from their illnesses.)

But most of us have no such guarantee. We're going to sludge along until our clocks stop (in seconds or 30 years or longer), so we have no excuse. What is tricky is working out the interrelated details with dependents.

For mates, both you and they should create a personal Action Plan. The financial resources will clearly overlap. Then get together and see how the plans can be made compatible and mutually supportive. A great tool for actual or potential conflict resolution is explained in Chapter 11 that can soften the edges and help synchronize goals for the exciting years ahead.

Dependents need their own Action Plan too, 40-plus or at any age.

Your children will, hopefully, be on their own by the time you hit 55, but if that is not the case then that special relationship must be factored into your Action Plan.

Whether you are single, joined, or otherwise encumbered, it's still *your* life and *your* time.

You do your own planning. Now.

Chapter 4

What is Inappropriate to Repeat the Second Time Around—and What is Essential?

If nature hadn't been in control those first 40 years, we'd all be as extinct as the puffed oozoo.

She had rules and a tight rein, but you outlasted her. You escaped—full of zest! You're free!

You can toss out the foolishness of the teens, forget the steam of "romantic love," quit leaping into bed just to prove you can, stop hunting for unconditional acceptance in all the wrong places, discontinue supporting your kids, and get rid of half your four-sizes-too-small wardrobe. Oh yes, the beauty contest has also ended—who cares?

Baggy boppers or sagging surfers don't cut it. It's time for something far more important than your species—you!

So what you need to know in this chapter is what is different in the post-40 years than before. What does freedom from nature really mean? What do we want to keep in our second lives? And what of the past is now simply an embarrassing waste of time and energy to repeat—and progressively less fitting as we truly mature?

Stop! Am I suggesting a Great Second Life without love, sex, or even rock-'n-roll? Why go on? Pass the vial. What could possibly replace them?

Real love, real sex, and maybe real music.

It's time to complete two guide lists, "In" and "Out," so we can pack appropriately for the liberating journey in the decades to come...

Why did we act like we did—and what we can toss overboard the second time around?

Too old for foolishness

The hardest period for most of us is from 40-55, when a mind-set honed in our earlier years to create adulation from peers and gratification any old way is suddenly the wrong notes to the wrong tune. We've outgrown the foolishness. We're dancing fools one day, regular fools the next.

What won hearts and accolades suddenly looks foolish. Where heads spun our direction, we've become instantly invisible. We were strutting down our road leading the pack. Now nothing looks familiar, and the only map we have points backwards.

Odder yet, as bewildered as we are, we don't really care all that much. If we could afford to be honest, or find anybody else who really cared or could understand, we'd admit that we're getting tired of the "youth game." The primping and posturing and the hustle suddenly aren't worth their salt.

Barbara Sher says it better

Nobody captures better the pain and retrospective humor of those first 40 years than Barbara Sher in *It's Only Too Late if You Don't Start Now*. She lived through them. She survived the hormonal mist. And now she provides a liberating map to freedom.

Let me summarize her retrospective look at us in nature's servitude.

Barbara says that the first 40 years aren't ours. That's when we pay our dues to nature. Our turn comes only when we get too old to breed. Having babies, being the fairest of the lot, and protecting our kids like crazy (until they give that craziness back to us) are the driving forces of youth. The bus stops are Beauty, Rebellion, Making It, and Doing It—is it any wonder we're frazzled by now? But a great transformation happens in the 40s when nature kicks us out.

Until then we are slaves to cultural narcissism. If you doubt it, look at when we were babies. When we were hungry, we screamed for food. When we were ignored or didn't get our way? More screaming. Our parents obeyed another mandate: they fed and loved us like we were the universe itself. Both were vital to keeping our species alive.

We relentlessly tried to hold on to that most-favored status that was the core of our first life. We learned that parents pulled back, others scowled, and eventually we couldn't be the center of everybody's existence, let alone that universe. But we never really gave up—until we had no choice. The game just changed. When puberty descended, we switched love fonts to the other sex. Nobody is to blame. It was a domino effect that ensured we would leave our childhood homes to find mates, reproduce as often as possible, and protect our children until they were old enough to do the same.

There is a biological purpose to this. The drama of this loss of unconditional love and our relentless struggle to get it back again is designed to save our species. That's why we compete obsessively with our siblings for attention. That's why we walk out on our unfair families at adolescence, in search of someone who will love us as we should be loved. That's why we try to be beautiful and successful and worthy of being adored again. That's also why we respond to the love our own infants feel for us—and only us—by falling madly in love with them.

And that's why we're thrown into panic at midlife, because we suddenly realize we're going to lose the battle. That we are mortal. The struggle to maintain some version of center stage is not only exhausting, we will lose.

The first 40 years belong to biology, not to us. And as we age and start to sag, spread, and lose hair, in comparison to others half our age, we're supposed to feel unhappy and try harder—we might just produce another baby!

Yet mankind has made huge technological advances. We simply stay younger and live longer than ever before—long after we are of any value to the species.

Something very curious happens during those years of enslavement. There are brief moments when we escape, when nature doesn't need us as badly. Three intermissions. The first is from the age of about 8 to 11, when we can take care of ourselves and become exceptional creatures, our most clear and creative selves, interested in friends, eager to learn. Then the hormones switch! The second intermission is somewhere in our twenties or early 30s, when we've found a satisfying love relationship, are married, and plan for or have babies. The third is after 40.

What do we have to look forward to in the third, open-ended intermission? Less beauty, less power, less status, less health, less love, less sex. (Or so nature thinks.) Then death.

Sounds awful.

But in fact it's a true blessing, a transformative time like no other that humans in the past have known. Another 30 or 40 years of freedom, unbound by nature, to be the best person we can.

And where might we look for insight into how the second life might be? To the 8-11 year-old, says Sher. An imp who wasn't afraid of either sex, who ran and cycled and let their body and mind roam. Who was funny, inquisitive, spirited. Who hadn't much use for money (since they seldom had any) and even less patience for pains and sickness.

Now it's time to capture the essence of that winged sprite, to find that creative center and to build from it. To find that amazing clarity and sense of self, an unconflicted ability to love learning, to experience unpossessive affection for friends... To let go of the craziness of the teen years and the head-down doggedness of the working years and regain control of the last years, to take into them the best of all the things we learned, to plan, then fulfill a Great Second Life from the moorings of the past.

How does this pertain to me and my second life?

We're crossing the Rubicon that separates our youth from our mature second life. We alone carry our future baggage, on tired shoulders and aching knees. We cross but once, so things must be left behind.

Here we make choices or *we* are left behind, a graying, anxious impostor who refuses to make the tribal cleansing required to become an elder.

One of the most difficult tasks of designing a truly personal Great Second Life is deciding what must be abandoned and which of the core values and dreams are consistent with post-breeding, full-adult maturity. Those we want to carry and nurture.

In Chapter Two we got a first glimpse of what we did in those first 40 years that we'd like to expunge now and in the future. On the "Me Now" Lists we wrote those adjectives and definitions that others (and we) might use to describe our first life. We noted the words identified with the earlier us that we don't want to perpetuate, and we described the attitudes, activities, and traits we want to leave on this side of the second life gate. (Many of those overlapped because, looking into the same well from different angles, we sometimes saw the same things.)

Later in this chapter we will focus even tighter on those things that can enhance our full enjoyment of the liberation that nature has unwittingly granted us—for living so long. We will create two personal guide lists to help us steer the course. What better titles than "In" and "Out"?

Now, let's take a no-nonsense, objective look at our first 40 (or 45, 50, or 55) years to determine which behaviors and thought patterns we want to keep and those that have run their course and no longer serve our present or future needs. We might also find behaviors that never were beneficial (and deserve to be excised immediately), plus other components so excessive that they must be questioned hard and let into our future only with clear restrictions and on a tight leash, if at all. (Drugs, booze, false pride, an outsized ego, overpowering sexuality, and perhaps smoking come immediately to mind.)

We will then list the behaviors that no longer work alongside those accomplishments, strengths, and positive personal traits we now possess and want to maintain, plus new strengths and traits we wish to create and develop in the years to come, to form the action outline of our Great Second Life.

Future accomplishments are less important. They will more likely come from life activities rather than from setting and achieving hard-and-fast goals. A second life for most will probably be less about seeking laurels and fattening dossiers than enjoyably being all that we can be (in mufti)—while having fun in the doing and growing. Less a future of "notches" than heart-felt feelings and smiles of satisfaction.

But we must be kind to ourselves when we look back at the moon surface of our past. We must delight in the peaks but not dwell unduly on the depths and prairies. Some of the less delightful sites had little to do with us. From what we did wrong or could have done better—the dumb choices, those secret caves of cowardice, the missed opportunities—we must learn the lessons they teach, then forget them. Nobody gets through the first 40 or 50 years unbruised. We must clean the slate as best we can. We get a second chance in a Great Second Life.

Loss?

What will we lose in our second life? Beauty and good looks, power and status, health, and love and sex. Then we get death.

Let's discuss each of them here, to see what baggage we can gratefully leave or discard on our journey into a new empire, where we are the emperor or empress.

Beauty and Good Looks

Nobody looks younger by growing older, except at the odd moments in our mind and heart. So what's the big deal? We'll have to surrender eventually. The only question is how.

We can respond in four ways to the bulging beltline or sagging skin.

We can resist with all our might. Gym junkies. Jazzercise. Tummy tucks. Face lifts. Chest hair implants. Liposuction. But what we can't buy is youth. We can just etch the illusion, then count the days.

We can yield slowly and strike a compromise with nature. Do what we can to preserve the activity and spunk of youth but respect time's calling. Stay in shape, eat healthful foods in modest quantities, switch to diet soda and low-cal dressing, protect ourselves from the sun, and keep a humor prod in hand to slow down nature's advances.

We can stop playing the game altogether, blend in, keep clean, and look elsewhere for more important values. Accept that aging is part of our heritage, take particular care of our minds and souls, keep our bodies fit and strong, and find new challenges to fill our days and nights.

Or we can go hog wild and not only yield to nature, become part of it. We can flee the normal conventions, toss our shoes, throw on a loin cloth, and slide back to the wild. The question is why.

"Easy for you to say!" you say, but who will love us when we look like our mother or father? Maybe ourselves, finally.

Beauty and good looks seem so superficial to be concerned about, but they aren't. In the U.S. we spent four billion dollars on our appearance in 2002. Part of us knows that we could better spend that money, time, and energy elsewhere. But a second part feels like another power is pulling our beauty strings—try as we may, they are completely out of our hands. Too many strands of the past, too much media and conditioning, are wrapped in how we look (or how we think others think we look) for us to quickly set them straight. The pretty people won the crowns and we were left to do the best we could with plain, damaged, or at best mediocre goods.

We learned to get by. We even got degrees, ran companies, wrote best sellers, and painted our way into museums while, we imagined, the pretty people married each other and posed. We did our best with what we had. But now even that is seeping away. There's only one consolation: we'll all be ugly in the end!

The saddest part is that all of it is such a waste. The only advantage nature wanted from the extra plumage and surface beauty was that we'd sire or have babies, and almost everybody had them anyway.

In our second life, new babies are rock bottom on anybody's list of priorities, at least new babies of our own. We're not as particular about siring.

So logic would suggest that the other skills and learning and values we gathered during our first life will be far more important the second time around, and that beauty and good looks will be reduced to health, vigor, cleanliness, and comfort.

That leaves us with the question, What do we leave behind as we begin our second life journey? Old thinking about the role of our appearance. Dressing to try to resurrect that "old you," or a you that you wish had existed. Clothes and body decoration that is blatantly inappropriate for who we are. Body deformation in the name of beauty.

What new attitudes do we embrace for the coming years? That we dress precisely how we feel and wish. If a boa, party dress, and slippers (or a T-shirt and a Zoot suit) make sense and would feel best, that's it—even to go shopping or renew a driver's license. That comfort is important, and what that means can change as our bodies change. That it's nobody's business but ours how we look and dress. But that we also won't use dress and appearance to intentionally embarrass ourselves or others, and if we do, we will find out what that is telling us and make needed modifications. Finally, that cleanliness is the minimum guide, for our own health, sense of well-being, and worth, as well as the comfort and concern of others.

Power and status

At some point in our Great Second Lives we will surely lose the power and status we now enjoy. But we will almost as surely acquire a new kind of serenity, which is a softer kind of personal power. And we might find new status too, if we want it.

Age doesn't necessarily diminish one's effectiveness or control. Popes have remained in power beyond their hundredth birthday, many acting heads of state ruled in their 80s, U.S. Presidents held office in their 70s, and the corporate world is dotted with chiefs 65+. Not to mention artists, writers, sculptors, architects, and others plying singular skills who performed at their peak far past their life expectancy. In some tribes you must be old before you can tell tribal stories. Only professional sports find active participants bowing out by 40 or thereabouts, knuckleball pitchers and Satchel Paige excepted.

In fact, in today's hectic world those at the top seldom get the luxury of thinking about relinquishing their power until they hit six score. In their 40s or 50s, while they may be easing into a new life phase in terms of beauty or love, they'll still need a full bag of business skills, plus the vigor to exercise them. Releasing power, or being released from it, for most comes with voluntary or forced retirement. Status can linger longer.

Perhaps the hardest part of having power and status is knowing when and how to give them up—or how to stop trying to retain them. Thus an important new element to add to our skill bag from about 40-50 on is an "exit plan," a set of steps that will let us continue to practice what we do best and enjoy most in a new arena, outside the direct employment realm or in a new job or firm.

We can also carry over the skills that create power and status into second life activities, like fund-raising and voluntary philanthropic or community-enhancing positions.

A related concern finds those with power and status so involved in reaching that position that they never develop extra-employment interests, hobbies, or even concerns. So when they find themselves unemployed and outside their comfort zone, they are lost. They have no place to reinvest their talents and energy. To offset this, then, another element to develop from 40 on are fields of interest where we can quickly shift when our last check is received and before the gold watch stops ticking.

There's more to say about power. Most of us aren't CEOs or moguls. We are everyday people somewhere in the cogs of business or are homemakers or run small companies or act on a stage. If we have mogul power, or much power at all, somebody forgot to tell us. Status? Only to the new hire or a new wife to whom anybody with more experience has status. That's unimportant. We still have the same kinds of stress, too many things to do in too little time, and pressure to achieve. We just want a break, some time somewhere to live and do what's important to us, or what should be important if we just had enough time to figure it out. And we suspect the moguls want the same thing.

We're hoping that the treadmill will at least slow down after we've learned the job, the kids are on their own, and our Great Second Life gets in gear.

Why wait that long? What we all share, hustling honchos and weary workers, is our obsession with control. As if we can somehow regulate the universe's throttle or alter the grander flow of life by our daily activities.

What we can do is affect our immediate universes in small ways. We can stand up for what's right. We can take action against greed and selfishness. But we're not omniscient, and we cannot do more than our best thoughts and actions which, if used as our guides, would bring us more personal acceptance and pride. It would inject far more reality and balance into our stressed worlds.

So what we might add to our skills-to-learn and perfect later would be a decided attempt to bring order and serenity to our present chaos. To do our best at all times, focus on the essentials, and learn to let the forces of life that do control kick in and do their part. Unless we are gods, that is our limit.

Then, when whatever power or status we have in others' eyes diminishes and our ego is disengaged, two true elements of lifelong happiness, clarity and serenity, will be in place to govern during our second life. And we will have had the benefit of honing and enjoying them in the meantime.

What don't we want to carry over the bridge? Obsession with control, chaos, self-inflicted stress, false gods, others' values, dishonest loyalty, irrational guilt, baseless anxiety, or any tendrils of shame.

Health

Health is so important that Chapter 6 is dedicated to it. The quality and length of our second life will be a direct result of our genetic inheritance, how we cared for ourselves in our first life, and what we do to maintain a healthy regimen in our coming days.

By health we mean the whole package, body and mind. So we will look in depth at what aging does to both, what we can modify at the gate, and where we should focus after 40.

For now, what, in summary, do we want in our second life? Everything sensible that will foster better health and a better, longer life.

Out? The reverse, particularly anything that we are doing in our 40s and 50s (and earlier) that will compromise our health and positive longevity.

Love and Sex

You thought we'd never get to the love and sex!

Actually, there's two kinds of love—let's call them "romantic love" and "true love"—and I suppose a thousand kinds of sex, but the generic (sometimes steamy) kind will do.

Romantic love is nature-driven, baby-producing, fleeting, usually heart-breaking, and certainly misnamed. Think teenagers and early twenties, though it lingers until the 40s or longer. Read passion, lust, "in love," hot sex, and maybe addiction.

True love usually comes later, can last forever, involves friendship, can also yield babies, and is even embraced by theologians. Sex too, as part of true love—sometimes hot but almost always more playful.

Let's use a left hand-right hand analogy.

The left hand stands for romantic love. This hand moves in one direction only, toward us, when we want to be loved. It grabs a mate and pulls them in. The criteria are few: a person who provides flesh for our private movies or dreams—what they lack in virtues or brilliance we will mentally provide. Barbara Sher says it best, "Romantic love (is) nothing but hunger, hormones, and illusion."

That it has a "mind of its own" is giving the left hand too much credit. There are no brain fibers there. It's granular, impetuous, relentless. And the results are wildly exciting and unforgettable, immortalized in song lyrics about impossibilities and unrequited yearning. It had better work. The propagation of our species depends on it.

When the left hand of "romantic love" starts wrinkling, shakes a bit, and becomes the topic of thinly-veiled bemusement by those a decade or two (or three) younger, every honest, red-blooded mortal knows what that hand has waiting for it: rejection, loneliness, a cold bed, and a drab, long life devoid of sparks and madness.

What foolishness. But we have to survive romantic love, infatuation, and fantasies gone wild to get to true love. Nature stuck it plunk in the way, plugged it in, and jumped aside.

Fortunately, it's on a timer, and at some point in our 40s the frenzy starts losing juice. We also get smarter the longer we live. We realize that one-way love (me, me, me) has a built-in flaw. Our lover wants me-me-me too. Since the left hand only takes, when romantic lovers don't get our undivided and continual love, they look elsewhere. The grabbing cycle starts over. It's exhausting, disappointing, and ultimately embarrassing as the hand gets slow and desperate. At some point we're too old for such foolishness. One-night stands and hit-and-score mates require too much energy, self-deception, money, and time.

Romantic love is the opposite of true love but sometimes a conversion takes place when the sex cloud lifts and we get to truly see and like the unique person we grabbed in passion and mated in haste.

The right hand represents true love. But it needs the left because it never works alone. Together, they reach out. They embrace their mate, and the world, because true love is more than sex, it's looking at others and life with our eyes and heart wide open. It's more than a fleeting orgiastic rush, it's a running high with another person or all people, with nature, with living, and with all of life.

But it can only happen when we slow down and know who we are. It requires the stability that maturity and having identified ourselves brings. When we come to realize our own worth, our singular value, we can then see the worth and value of other people and things. We love them simply for what they are, not as we want them to be. By comparison, the high drama and electric pizzazz of romantic love shows its true colors: neon bizarre. Unplug it and there's nothing there but the echo of sizzle.

In true love we will only stay with people we like. And if we like ourselves and what we see around us, we will no longer feel that hollow, aching loneliness that romantic love always brought when the fire died. We will reach out to life to find companionship, selecting those we want near us. We will become a self-sustaining core of a radiant universe, and will want those by us to experience their own radiance as much as share ours. We will have enough love stored up to select friends. We won't need fantasies to fill in the human gaps.

There is something magnetic about people who know what they want, can choose, say no kindly but firmly, and who exude joy, curiosity, and goodness. That's who we can be when we switch from romantic to true love.

If true love sounds as bland as pale pasta, what it lacks in flash it makes up in stability and permanence, which are the strongest building blocks of a contented second life.

Fortunately, sex can remain as integral a factor as it was for romantic love, but seldom its white-hot core and often only element. It's sex at a different pace. Nothing to prove, no performance expectations. Sex to be enjoyed. Playful. Love-laden.

The myth is that with age goes the sexual desire. Humbug, says James Firman, president of the National Council on Aging in discussing a 1998 study on the topic. "For many older Americans, sex remains an important and vital part of their lives."

According to that NCOA survey, 48% of Americans 60+ engage in sexual activity at least once a month. (The percentage would have been higher had more partners been available. There are five times as many widows as widowers in those totals. Plus 13% of the men and 44% of the women had partners with a medical condition that prevented them from having sex.) Moreover, 74% of the sexually active men and 70% of the sexually active women said they are as satisfied or even more satisfied emotionally with their sex life than they were in their 40s.

So what do we leave, internally kicking and in high dander, at the gate of a Great Second Life? The mindset and exhausting demands of romantic love. The conquest tallies; hot sheets; game-playing; sweaty risk-taking with AIDs, herpes, and other consequences; lies; pierced hearts, and the flat-out danger and all the high drama and tingle that brings.

What do we take with us, or acquire when nature turns down the voltage or we learn to override it? Lovers who talk and share, close friends who are extra-libidinous, personal contentment with who we are, the ability to say no, an eagerness to enjoy the coming years on our and life's terms, plus open eyes and an even more accepting heart.

The hardest time is indeed from about 40-55, when we still have the body, more cunning, and finally the money to play the romantic game we fumbled at and scrimped through in youth. Nature holds on with a hook, shouting "one last baby while you still can!" And while we're not too anxious about the baby, the sex still burns bright—while we still can, certain that at any moment both the desire and the ability will flee and we'll suddenly be as able, interested, and sexy as a crinkled troll.

We're half right. The desire will decrease, as much from the realization that the capture is no longer worth the hunt, and that there's another life awaiting us that simply makes more sense and is better designed to our maturing bodies and minds. Those transition years are hard ones. As much as we may try to talk ourselves out of hot sex, nature may pull us back.

But eventually it happens, then real love can too. We get other valuable second life gifts too: real friends, real sex, and more truth, honesty, and reality.

Death

If you do everything suggested in this book, you will still die. (The same will happen if you don't.) That's the nature of our beast. Sorry.

But what a run we mortals get! We get to experience love, acceptance, joy, surprise, success, happiness, even patches of ecstasy. We get to know wonderful people, see the world, run, swim, fly, ski, laugh, drive, dream, write, and read.

Of course, we don't have much say about what we do or how we are treated early on, and there are times when survival takes first call, but there are also long periods during our lives when we can direct our actions and mold our immediate environment. We can always expand our minds.

We probably have more opportunity to be our fullest and best selves during our second lives, when the rages of youth abate and wisdom (or at least experience) alights.

A goal of this book is to help you extract every advantage and joy from that Great Second Life, so when Death does come knocking, your slate and your heart will be full, without regrets at what is still left undone.

Ours is a spectacular but finite world. We get one dance ticket, then the music stops. Dance!

Guide Lists: "In" and "Out"

In Chapter Two we took a first look at our lives now, what we like and don't like. We even filled in some provisional lists, to help us clarify those thoughts.

Now we want to look more seriously at what we want to discard from our present, scattered holdings and what we want to carry into our second life, or add to it when we are there.

These are basic things, core life things. Later, we will add a Dream List of specific actions or activities we want to pursue. We will also have looked at both our health and our financial status to see what means, and restrictions, we have to make those dreams a reality.

Here we are talking more about the kind of person we would like to be, the signposts we want on our trail of daily living. To help us, we have taken a quick look at beauty, power and status, health, and love and sex. (We needn't add death to either list. The reaper always gets the last laugh.)

Time to complete more lists!

On the "In" list, write down those things, actions, traits, and thoughts you want to carry to and build from during your second life.

Conversely, put on the "Out" list anything you don't want continued from your life now (or even started later).

Like all of the lists in this book, these can be modified at will, and can be as long as you wish. (You may wish to look again at your "Me Now" lists in Chapter 2 for any ideas and insights they provide.)

Some thinking helps here, so a good way to prepare the lists is to write down the obvious items first, then add more in the minutes, hours, or days that follow, as they occur to us. Copy the lists and work on them in the off hour, adding the new items to the master list later. If done by hand, recording in pencil makes sense while the wording is finalized; then pen.

SECOND LIFE "IN" LIST

What you want to include in your Great Second Life:

1.	
2.	
3.	
4.	
5.	
6.	
7.	
8.	
9.	
10.	
11.	
12.	
13.	
14.	
15.	
16.	
17.	
18.	
19.	
20.	

If this is a library book, please do not fill in this page! For a free, full-page download of this form, see www.super-second-life.com/form4A.htm

SECOND LIFE "OUT" LIST

What you want excluded from your Great Second Life:

1.	
2.	
3.	
4.	
5.	
6.	
7.	
8.	
9.	
10.	
11.	
12.	
13.	
14.	
15.	
16.	
17.	
18.	
19.	
20.	

If this is a library book, please do not fill in this page! For a free, full-page download of this form, see www.super-second-life.com/form4B.htm

Reading Sources

Bortz II, Walter M., M.D., *Dare to be 100: How to Live Long and Enjoy it to the Fullest.* (Fireside, 1996). In Chapter 5, the "Gameplan," is particularly interesting. Also see his *Longer Living for Dummies* (For Dummies, 2002).

Carter, Jimmy, *The Virtues of Aging.* (Ballantine, 1998). An excellent account of the former President and wife Rosalynn's coming to grips with their second lives.

Dowling, Colette, *Red Hot Mamas: Coming into Our Own at 50.* (Bantam, 1996). Very funny: addresses sex, money, hormones, and menopause. For mamas of any temperature.

Dychtwald, Ken, *Age Wave.* (BantamDoubledayDell, 1990). An early, important book in the field. Good facts showing the power and numbers of those who are or will be seniors. Also read his *Age Power: How the 21st Century Will Be Ruled by the New Old* (J.P. Tarcher, 2000).

Ellis, Dave, *Creating Your Future.* (Houghton Mifflin, 1998). An easy system to follow.

Ferrin, Kelly, *What's Age Got to Do With It? Secrets to Aging in Extraordinary Ways.* (Alti, 1999). Need inspiration? 101 biographies of old folks living fully.

Marc Freedman, *Prime Time: How Baby Boomers Will Revolutionize Retirement and Transform America.* (Public Affairs, 2002).

Kaplan, Lawrence J., *Retiring Right: Planning for Successful Retirement.* (Square One Publishers, 2002).

Leshan, Eda, *It's Better to Be Over the Hill Than Under It: Thoughts on Life Over 60.* (Newmarket Press, 1992. For women; insightful and very funny. A journalist with a magic pen.

Oxford Book of Aging. (Oxford Press, 1994). What the older think of aging.

Perls, Thomas T., et al, *Living to 100: Lessons in Living to Your Maximum Potential at Any Age.* (Basic Books, 2000).

Pipher, Mary, *Another Country: Navigating the Emotional Terrain of our Elders.* (Riverhead Books, 2000). Great insights and interviews.

Pogrebin, Letty Cottin, *Getting Over Getting Older: An Intimate Journey.* (Berkley Pub. Group, 1997). Focuses on what really counts. Very well written, with much humor. Again, for women.

Ready or Not Retirement Guide, 2003. (Manpower Education Institute).

Rivers, Joan, ***Don't Count the Candles: Just Keep the Fire Lit***. (HarperCollins, 2000). Funny.

Sheehy, Gail, ***New Passages: Mapping Your Life Across Time***. (Random House, 1996). Gail has some newer spin-offs of this book, with update data, but this is the core book for the 50+ (as she reached 50). A very good chapter about the "Flourishing Forties" too. She's a journalist with a sociological bent. Her examples are inspiring. See her listing of 11 books about menopause; Sheehy wrote the key book on the topic.

Sher, Barbara, ***It's Only Too Late if You Don't Start Now: How to Create Your Second Life at Any Age.*** (Delacorte Press, 1999). My favorite book to get your head right with aging. Better yet, it's funny and full of useful exercises to throttle the 40-55 tremors. Sher has other good books too—and she's older than you are!

Walker, Barbara, ***Create Your Retirement: 55 Valuable Ways to Empower the Rest of Your Life***. (Trafford, 2002).

For a list of aging-related general organizations (with address, phone, and website), please see the Appendix.

"Life was meant to be lived, and curiosity must be kept alive. One must never, for whatever reason, turn his back on life."

Eleanor Roosevelt

Chapter 5

How Do You Plan for a Three-Tiered Great Second Life?

Your second life is really divided into three parts: the emotionally difficult 40-55 year period; the proactive, dynamic second segment, and the reactive, reflective third.

Ideally, during the first 15 years you set the table for your second life. The second period is when most, perhaps all, of that second life takes place. The third consists of those few years (or months) when you lose independence, when comfort and survival replace growth and adventure. Some never experience the third segment at all.

This chapter focuses on defining that three-tiered reality. It also proposes that the relationships, interests, and activities pursued in the first 40 or so years make the three tiers that follow more enjoyable and eventful as well.

Ideally, the three segments seamlessly segue to create a Great Second Life

---

The First Tier: 40-55 Years of Age

It seems a bit askew, if not grossly unfair, to ask us to launch a "second life" plan when we are just reaching the peak of our "first life," during the high-powered years from 40-55. That's when we hit full maturity and statistically we earn our top dollar, when our kids are growing up and our responsibility buckets are overflowing, and when we have become our own person—or should.

But, as we've already seen, they are troubled years too. Nature is getting ready to pull the plug when they start, and has left us to our wiles by the time they end. We're no longer kids, but we're not creaking old either.

We're standing in the middle of the bridge between youth and age, having seen mortality—our own—on the horizon, a horizon that doesn't look all that far away.

The Middle Years

Not surprisingly, I call these the "middle years." Not only do they fall chronologically near our mortal 50-yard line, they are also the time when our vigor, health, and performance are prime. When we have conquered the ignorance and innocence of youth but are still unfettered by the debilitation of age.

It's then we can most influence the kind of second life we might have during our later years.

Most of the money we will save for the future will be set aside to compound then, unless we were wise enough to begin earlier. It may also be our last chance to significantly make up for undersaving.

It's the time when our health-related patterns start digging in. Fifteen years of hard drinking and heavy smoking then can dramatically reduce both the length and quality of the second period—and of our lives in general. Conversely, that's when regular exercise, a healthy diet, and close attention to our weight and to early ailments and conditions can markedly increase the length and quality of the years to follow.

This is the time when we strengthen the bonds and friendships with our families and friends that can infuse joy and sharing in the coming Great Second Life. Links that can help create a buffer against a lonely, isolated old age.

By 55 we have also created an interest reservoir from which we can draw all the years to follow. After the frenetic sports and motion of youth, a new kind of exploration emerges during the "middle years." We find different things that we enjoy doing, seeing, hearing, reading, and trying; they whet our appetites for fuller, deeper examination and later pursuit when we have more time, fewer distractions, and less pressing responsibilities.

We begin our Second Life Action Plan during the "middle years."

Financially, it makes the most sense—and cents—to start promptly at 40 (if not 20) to lay out the way and means by which we can finance a comfortable later and old age. Also, to initiate the kind of lifelong health regimen that will allow us to extract from the body, and life itself, all that you wish and it can provide.

When you start your dream list and begin to plot the framework of your Great Second Life is less time-intensive. Like deciding when you will no longer be a kid, the day will come. It will speak firmly: "What am I going to do from now on?" If not sooner, I'd look for it about the time the big "5-0" falls, when pregnancy and signing that million-dollar sports contract just aren't going to happen.

But if no voice beckons, what better way to celebrate a 50+ birthday than by getting to work looking ahead on paper.

If your mind decides that it WILL NOT PLAN a second life (rebellious minds speak in capital letters), you have two choices. You can scold it firmly ("You are responsible for your own life, dummy. You're going to let others do that? Or fate?") Or don't: you'll still live on, though it may be more haphazard and less fun.

The Second Tier: 55 Plus

The only certainty of the second tier is that we arbitrarily start it after 55. It may end at 56, or 96, or it may never really end, with our last breath being that of a vigorous, independent person.

The second tier closely parallel's Dr. Mary Pipher's "young-old" group in *Another Country: Navigating the Emotional Terrain of Our Elders*. I call these the "discerning years." They are the extra time given us to use the keen judgment, insight, or perception we gathered from our work, learning, and play during our first 55 years, plus any additional acumen we gather as we continue to learn and grow.

The purpose of the Action Plan is to provide guidance and intellectual support to those passing through the second and third tiers. It creates key touchpoints for those in the "discerning years," and keeps the control of their lives firmly in their hands.

The Action Plan is a rough guideline always subject to further refinement and modification. It is indeed a map to a personal territory only vaguely perceived when entered, and never fully finalized. A map in progress, it allows us to explore in any direction, filling in the details and suggested activities as it is being created and experienced.

Yet, as humans, we know about other humans who have been or are now in the land of the 55-plus. And we can project ourselves, and our wishes and dreams, on what we see and know about them. Thus planning at 40 or 50 for life at 60 or 80 is possible, though approximate.

An Action Plan that helps those 55+ maximize the use of their time, knowledge, skills, resources, and energy to enjoy a Great Second Life is what we seek.

Those in the "discerning years" will be the greatest beneficiaries if that is attained. That can bring benefits to others too: the children (and parents) of those in the "discerning years" who, like the rest of society, will see older citizens in control of full, productive lives, doing what they want to do by intent rather than happenchance, able to redesign their lives when and as they wish.

The Third Tier

The sorrow is that for most there must be a third tier, a buffer time between full independence, control and, alas, death.

Yet this needn't be a sad time, simply one in which we are less physically proactive and more directed to comfortably enjoying life on a daily basis.

I call these the "reflective years," the time to both think back and resonate on the achievements of a life fully lived, and to appreciate those who have been positively guided and helped by what we have done during our short earthly sojourn.

This is the period when we must call upon others to help provide support, to guide us in the areas where we have lost our independence. It is where we share what we know and have learned with our grandchildren, children, other family members, and friends.

A Great Second Life doesn't end the moment one enters this final phase of life. What one enjoyed before, they can usually, with adaptations, continue to enjoy now. The friendships gathered throughout life become more precious in the "reflective years," and often a great serenity prevails, a contentment at having done so much and been so blessed.

This is when the financial planning many years back is most appreciated, when the ability to earn is gone but costs continue. The peace at knowing that both the earlier planning and modest sacrifice now lift the burden of the costs from family, friends, or society is a particular reward of an Action Plan well executed.

So What?

Who cares if there are three or 20 tiers, and what has that to do with us?

It helps us put and keep our mental house in order by having a rational toehold on life's patterns. And it provides a logical schedule to do things when they are best done.

Tier one is when we best put the plans for a second life in motion, and adjust our actions accordingly. Tier two, the "discerning years," are when most of our active second life takes place.

Yet it's never too late to enjoy a well deserved Great Second Life. If you're 88, new to the concept and clamoring at the bit, get going!

Chapter 6

What Will You Do About Your Physical and Mental Health?

If we are to believe the barrage of "good news" dotting the press daily (about doubling our life expectancy, DNA, magic pills, and turtles that don't age), we may all live to be 200— if we can just hang on a few more weeks. So what's to worry?

We'd better address this myth before we tackle present-day, flesh and bone reality!

We had also better focus on our own and our contemporaries' current and coming physical and mental health, on the long shot that corporeal immortality arrives after we've caught the last train. Without either in full temper, getting old will really be a climb to reach that leave-taking terminal.

Once we see what and where we are physically and mentally, let's implement a four-step process to gain some sense of control, in case some dreaded, adverse anomalies come knocking, uninvited and unwanted.

That is logically followed by a broader look at what physically awaits most seniors, at least in North America. There are physical ailments and conditions that appear with age. Other ailments and conditions, more opportunistic, may dash through the door the moment we open it. So we might begin a concerted campaign to hold them at bay, or remove the precursory conditions that increase the likelihood of their unwelcome entrance. Alas, some are totally out of our hands: they are gifted to us genetically. For all, this look will at least provide a pinch of understanding, to lessen the shock of seeing their new face.

A similar, broad look at our coming mental state, with its emotional and psychological components, will deal more with myths and truths than suggest steps by which we might somehow jack up our IQ another 50 points or remember our pharmacist's phone number (or location).

Then we must put all of this knowledge and information to work so we can fully use what we have to create our own very best second life. That will include synchronizing the use of our abilities while we have them to realize our dreams. Let's wait until the next chapter to create some understanding of the money and protective tools, like insurance and assistance, that we will need to be safeguarded into old old age while not being a burden on family or friends. Stress is indeed a killer; all of this may help reduce that stress.

Good health is important to a Great Second Life

Ground rules and two myths

When we speak of a second life, aging, and health, we need a set of overriding ground rules. One, we are mortal. Two, it isn't a sin to die, but it may be not to live.

So our purpose here is to both administer and enjoy our health as well and as fully as possible so we live the best life we can.

Let's set aside two myths: old doesn't equal sick, nor, by extension, does getting older mean getting sicker. In 1994, of Americans 75-84, 73% reported no disability. Even those over 85, 40% were fully functional. And the reduction in disability is accelerating, even among those over 95.

The second is that we are all headed for the nursing home. Hardly. Only 5.2% of the populace resides in nursing homes at any one time, and while over 40% will be there at some point in their lives, many of those spend only their last days or months there before dying.

Our focus in this chapter, then, is to take a good look at our present health, how that might change as we age, and how we factor those changes into our second life plans. While disability and nursing homes might be part of those last 30 years, so will decades of full, fun living with health very much in the background. Those years are our primary concern.

Of course, if our physical and mental health aren't functioning well at any age, the rest of our life directly suffers—and it may be prematurely shortened. So most of what follows are things we can do *now* to get our body, our mind, and our attitude in as good a shape as possible, so that we can fully enjoy our bonus years.

But first we should also address the "why worry?" issue, that it doesn't matter what we do, scientists are about to unveil the life-stretcher, the pill or system that will keep us all healthy and hopping until we're 200—or was that 500?—years old.

Living to 200—or much longer

Live three times as long as our grandparents? A mixed blessing. Who wants to live two days longer if they are throbbing with uncontrollable, permanent pain or have the mind and future of a wrinkled potato? And who among us saved up enough survival money for two or three lifetimes?

On the other hand, with a much longer midlife and a long, enjoyable later life, given the resources and energy to do what we enjoy every day, hooray for those life-stretchers! Just think, if those 200 years were run in reverse, we'd still be able to speak with Thomas Jefferson.

But will you and I live to be 200? Fat chance. At best, we can watch with interest as science pulls forward both the fully functional length and the absolute length of life for those who follow—maybe for our grandchildren. It will be fun to watch, and if it touches us a bit, great! Right now most of us begin to suffer significant reduced function at about 70 while our absolute length is about 120.

Of course, we can already extend our lives by both paying attention to our health and by courting daily the forces that support longer life—mostly by cutting our vices and through adding a healthy diet, exercise, vigorous mental activity, and less stress (with a few magic pills thrown in). We can also hope that the forces that foster longer life appear quickly and work fast enough so we can ride their coattails. Maybe some of them will at least reverse our bodily damage—that tasted so good to inflict.

What are the changes to look for (and coattails to grab)?

◆ Some of the changes relate to stress, environment, and the body's ability to repair itself. Some animals don't deteriorate much at all, in safe, stressless settings. Rock fish live 150 years. We must adapt to humans what we can learn from them.

◆ Scientists can now double the life span of fruitflies by simply focusing on natural selection. The task is finding the genes involved, then applying pharmacology and gene replacement. When understood, reweaving the human genetic fiber will control the aging, which will allow us to stay healthier, younger, and able to fully function much longer.

◆ Those eating foods lower in calories, much less fat, and high in nutrients may live 1/3 longer, if animal studies on rats and monkeys hold true in humans. We will be younger physiologically and have more stamina, better immune systems, and fewer diseases, according to Drs. Rick Weindruck from the University of Wisconsin, Madison, and UCLA's Roy Walford.

◆ Less glucose also seems to be a longevity key, says Dr. Anthony Cerami (formerly from Rockefeller University), in part since it is also a protection against diabetes (which accelerates aging by a third). Since glucose causes harm when reacting with proteins, less glucose reduces the stiffening of joints, toughening of bones, and function loss in organs. A new compound breaks the damaging cross-linking, which is one of the causes of aging.

◆ Oxygen free radicals are atoms or molecules with at least one unpaired electron, and thus are usually reactive and unstable. That's bad news in humans since they are often linked to cancer. They also attack the mitochondria's membranes and thus destroy us as we age. What can we do now? According to SMU's Dr. Raj Sohal, eat fruits and vegetables and exercise!

◆ Dr. Miriam Nelson, from Tufts, speaks of a "magic pill," a growth hormone for use in later life to stop the loss of body strength. It will bring more muscle, less fat, and more vitality, which in turn creates a sexier, stronger, more energized person. Beware, though: one side effect is cancer.

◆ Turn back the aging clock? Yes, says Dr. Judith Campesi from UC. Berkeley. "If we can reset the clock in each cell by lengthening the telemeres, they can divide without limit and we can abolish aging altogether!" What happens now when the cells stop dividing? We wrinkle, our skin ages, and we can't fight disease. The solution is to restore the cells' function(s) once they stop dividing.

Are we doomed to wait for the new bullet train while riding our old coal burner until the coal runs out? Hardly.

The smartest thing we can do is what we are doing now—planning, then living the greatest second life possible, without losing time standing by the tracks and pining about what may be at best a mixed blessing.

Remember that our kin just a bit more than a century back lived an average of 48 years. Hard years, without antibiotics, cars, airplanes, radio, television, the computer, aspirin, or sanitary napkins. They too dreamed of a life when most people lived to 75 and some to 100. They wondered who would benefit from such wonders. Us, that's who. Our train goes twice as far as theirs and much faster. We just have to live the journey fully.

But there's more. We can actually extend our lives today by our personal actions, by what we do, eat, and think. Let's first look at where we are now physically and mentally, then see where we can pick up some extra coal to keep our old buggies chugging a bit longer.

The status of our physical and mental health first

The first thing we have to do is determine where we are physically and mentally. Little of this is a mystery—who knows us better than ourselves? Who else feels our pains? So some of this is simply establishing a baseline, part by part, for future comparison, much as a doctor does on an initial physical exam.

To that we must add some family history, to at least be aware of areas where future attention may be drawn.

And then we must get a second opinion, in this case from our physician, to begin a life maintenance program designed to keep us healthy, active, and fully involved all our days.

The idea is to be proactive physically and mentally now, with a four-step opening volley, then work our actions into an everyday routine that becomes part of our lifetime maintenance program. The kick-off action steps, according to Ken Dychtwald, are:

1. If it hurts, pinches, oozes, swells, or smells, **give it immediate attention**. Get it under control now; then, if possible, get it cured.

2. If it's been lingering around and is correctable, **get it evaluated** and under treatment.
3. If it's been around "forever" (and is chronic), **get it under control** and keep it there, and
4. As each new health concern arises, **treat it promptly**.

The point is obvious: we should enter our second life armed with both health knowledge and a proactive plan to be able to enjoy every day fully and actively. We must get beyond the obsessive certainty that something will appear without warning and do us in. Or the worse mindset that "if I ignore it, it will go away." Either can happen, but the best armor is information, professional input, and healthy living.

So that requires a personal checklist for us to complete, then share with our physician. It can be as informal as starting with our toes and moving up, noting anything of concern now or in the past at each way station: a knee that "pops out" when we walk, a sagging libido, a lip sore that has lingered for weeks or months. Then list the senses: sight, hearing, smell, taste, and touch. Anything unusual there? We take this list to our exam and discuss each item to see if it falls into the four action categories above or if it is at the initial, flag-waving stage where subsequent changes will merit attention or treatment.

To that list we add a dozen or so categories that must also be addressed, and should be checked annually, by our physician as we age: alcohol, drug, and tobacco use and abuse; breast cancer concerns; decline in function; deconditioning; hearing problems; dental problems; high blood pressure; malnutrition; vision problems; thyroid disease; prostate disease, and depression—plus any of the others discussed later in this chapter.

The list is also incomplete without factoring in our earlier health record and our family health pattern. As well, women who have not had regular exams must include a check for cervical cancer. Those of us with significant sunlight exposure now or in the past should have a skin cancer check. Heavy drinkers and smokers should check for oral cancer. And if there are indications or family history in colon cancer or diabetes mellitus, that should be checked too. Possible coronary heart disease should make everybody's checklist. And for the old old, so should obesity, dementing illness, and abuse or neglect.

A quick summary of our family's health must accompany our personal checklist when given to the doctor. Of particular concern is the health of our parents, grandparents, and siblings. What major health problems do or did they have, when did they begin, and what was the result of each. Of obvious concern are genetic hand-downs, but also a shared environment can indicate possible future health concerns we shouldn't overlook. This is not a list of impending doom but rather a peek at answers to future questions that might arise.

To our personal list and the family health record, we should add anything else of consequence in the health arena. This is the moment to clean the slate of all our preoccupations, then let our physician decide what deserves instant attention, what will be monitored, what we can do to improve our present state and keep it functioning well, and which other professionals or experts might be brought in to confront specific needs. This is also where we work with the doctor to create an ongoing, positive second life health maintenance plan. (Bring this book if your doctor has no idea what we're talking about!)

Why bother with all of this? Why not just live it up and take our chances later? Because by exploring our health future now, correcting the present malfunctions before they grow and worsen, and adding in the record from several generations past, we might well be able to improve our chances of a long, pain-free, active future rather than reactively having to counter whatever we are dealt.

What must we do to maintain good physical health?

It's not enough just to get a baseline evaluation. We must also put ourselves on a life-enhancing and -extending health regimen, if we want to enter and enjoy a healthy and long second life. That doesn't mean 30 years of sprouts, cold showers, and endless push-ups. But it does mean paying attention to simple, sensible acts that will make us more agile and able to do what we want longer.

One way to view this is to look backward. What are the seven habits of people who live 100+ years?

1. sleep 7-8 hours a night
2. eat breakfast
3. don't eat between meals
4. keep their weight between 5% below and 10-20% above normal for their size
5. get regular physical activity
6. imbibe no more than two alcoholic drinks daily
7. don't smoke

And for us, who will gladly settle for most of those 100 years? We've already seen that eating food lower in calories and fat, plus favoring fruits and vegetables, are key components in programs that help eliminate free radicals and may extend our lives by a third. So one area where we can focus now and into the future is our **diet**.

Are there guidelines to determine what is a sensible diet? As many as there are nutritionists and diet-sellers. But a few have stood the tests and time. We can determine a healthy weight for ourselves (say 150 pounds), multiply that by ten, and keep our food intake within that many calories (1500), plus the number we expend in exercise (if, for example, we cycle 200 calories worth, to maintain our weight we get to ingest 1700 calories worth of food that day).

What kind of food? Keep the saturated fat a very small percentage of that total. Whole grains, fruits, and vegetables are low in calories and fat and are excellent components of any meal. We should limit the salt we add, and women may need more calcium and iron, before menopause. Beyond that, personal needs may require special dietary modifications. An example is the care that diabetics must take to maintain a proper insulin balance.

Alcohol can be a problem when used in excess. (In some, one drink is excessive.) Alcoholism in older people carries a toll, including proneness to injury (at a time when bodies mend slower and secondary complications appear), gastrointestinal illness, liver disease, malnutrition, and sometimes dementia.

Two-thirds of the chronic, excessive drinkers are longtime drinkers, but they are hardly a second life concern since most are dead by 65. At 40 we should be putting the brakes on our drinking. The other third are situational drunks; their addiction can be exacerbated by the things that age can bring, like retirement, money worries, health problems, and the death of loved ones.

There's a direct link between alcoholism, depression, and impotence, which makes it harder for alcoholics to even want to live a healthy, exciting second life, much less adhere to a healthy life style to make it happen. Women aren't excluded either; after 40, they are affected more quickly by alcohol. When should we seek help with our drinking? If the alcohol affects our relationships, influences how we schedule our days, alters our health, isolates us, or simply preoccupies us.

Exercise is very important in preventing health problems, including cardiovascular disease and depression, although less than 25% of Americans exercise at all. How beneficial? Walk an hour a day—it needn't be all at one time—and you will live two more years. Women who exercise an hour daily will cut their risk of breast cancer by a third.

Building muscle, according to Dr. Nelson, may be the most important thing older folks can do to lengthen their lives and sharpen their mental acuity. As we age, we gain weight and lose muscle strength, but the latter can be reversed in as little as two months. Simple strength and endurance exercises can be done by either sex at any age; it stops free radicals as a bonus.

The minimum goal is some type of sustained activity for 30-40 minutes at least three times a week. We needn't run marathons, scale peaks, or swim to the Azores, but the body continues to crave exercise, and it rewards us accordingly.

Dr. Mark E. Williams, in *The Complete Guide to Aging and Health*, says it best:

> Regular exercise is the best antidote to many of the effects of aging. The major benefits from regular exercise include favorable effects on fats in the blood, better handling of blood sugar, increased maximal oxygen capacity, greater strength, denser bones, an improved sense of well-being, and better sleep.

Smoking has deservedly received a bum health rap these past years, and anybody who doesn't know that it is harmful to their health probably *is* one of those aliens we see in movies living in human bodies. So if we're resisting with all of our might, puffing into our second life is a luxury we can ill afford. In a nutshell: it's far more likely to painfully shorten than extend those extra years.

Alas, the body is more forgiving than society. Quit now and in two to five years our elevated risk of heart disease is about equal to a non-smoker. The risks of cancer and emphysema also drop markedly. Circulation improves. Friends return. Insurance rates drop. And we aren't reminded daily that cigarette smoking remains the single most preventable cause of death in the United States for men and women and that we can cure 85% of all cancer if people (like us) stopped smoking.

The last thing we can do to extend our life and make it more enjoyable is to reduce our **stress**. Stress is the body's response to a demand, and too much stress has physical and psychological consequences, including insomnia, headaches, and ulcers. It wears the body down and reduces the amount of repair the body makes to itself, which induces aging.

There are solutions—and good news: we experience less stress as we age! We can simply stop worrying so often, at least about things over which we have no control. Earthquakes, conspiracies, the falling ruble, even bad jokes happen but beyond taking prudent precautions and remaining attentive, the stress we develop about them and other uncontrollable actions serves no useful purpose. Healthy coping mechanisms to stress include exercise, meditation, biofeedback, or self-hypnosis; unhealthy ones include overeating and substance abuse.

What you are doing now—planning a full, active, enjoyable second life—may be the very best way to reduce stress. You are taking control and creating your own future reality. Since you are the creator, if things don't work out, no stress—just change the reality!

Living long enough to enjoy a Great Second Life does have health consequences beyond those just mentioned. Everyday things change because of age. These are the most common examples that we must consider now and factor into our future plans:

◆ The third addiction (after tobacco and alcohol) is **drugs**. Not many dedicated cocaine or heroin users reach middlessence. A bigger concern are the old-fashioned, doctor-prescribed legal drugs. Not every user is addicted and some simply must use them to live those extra years with any pleasure, but the guess is that about 60% of the 50+ users are needlessly addicted to painkillers, tranquilizers, sedatives, sleeping pills, or muscle relaxants.

◆ Let's look at **depression** again because it is so common in seniors and is an organic illness with biochemical changes in the body. It's estimated that 25% of the seniors dip into depression at some point, and that 1/3 of those with dementia probably are depressed and are treatable. The treatment for depression is specific drugs and psychotherapy, one or both. Sometimes it passes on its own in six months—but what a lousy, hopeless six months. Dangerous too, because the depressed can turn to suicide. Particularly vexing to seniors is the depression created by mixing alcohol with specific allergy medicines, antidepressants, barbiturates, motion sickness medication, painkillers, sleeping pills, and some blood pressure prescriptions.

◆ Let's talk **sex**, again. It can be a vital element of a Great Second Life, or so thought 97% of 800 folks 60-91 years old in a study that said they liked sex. Eighty percent thought it was good for their health. But **impotence** can soften that enthusiasm real fast! Yet 50-60% of the 10 million men thus afflicted have a physical cause that can be treated. Prescription drugs can be one of those possible causes. There are 41 that can be implicated, including Tagamet, Desyrel, Prozac, and Valium—plus, of course, alcohol and tobacco.

◆ **Prostate enlargement** starts appearing in the 40s and will be present in virtually all men by about 65. Three things to consider: (1) get a PSA blood test often to make sure it doesn't become cancerous; (2) exercise and sex help in the short run ("Head for the bed, Mabel. My prostate's acting up!"), and (3) there are effective drugs now to use before or instead of surgery.

◆ If we can keep our **heart** in shape, bingo—that's the #1 killer in folks over 50. So we need to get our blood pressure checked and treated if it's too high, watch our cholesterol levels, pay attention to our diet (or start one) if we're more than 20% over our ideal body weight, and exercise regularly.

◆ **Menopause** used to be a hint to get coffin insurance. Now women live a third of a great life with and after menopause. Some see it as the gateway to an exciting new beginning, but the passing can be unpleasant: 75% of the women have symptoms. Most are immediately treatable. Menopause can also create a new, positive, dynamic in a marriage. It's also a time to see your physician—to hear the newest thoughts about hormone replacement therapy and to learn more about preventing osteoporosis.

◆ Women jump into the fore for **heart disease** after menopause, so weight is an issue. Attention to eating matched with exercise can usually remove this concern.

◆ What fun is a second life if we're as blind as Magoo? By 45, most of us need corrective lenses; almost all do by 60. So we need to get our **eyes** checked, in part for macular degeneration. (While there, have a glaucoma check. Two million people have it and half don't know.) If cataracts are found, 95% of those with them had improved vision after surgery. And forget tinted lenses or sunglasses at night after we're 60: we need seven times the light that a 20 year-old requires. There are also amazing laser eye surgeries that quickly correct near- and far-sightedness.

◆ If our **hearing** is getting worse, guess what, it happens with age, mostly to men. (A quick cure: move to the African Sudan, where there is no hearing loss.) Unfortunately, the range most affected includes the human voice. The single greatest cause? Excessive earwax! Some need surgery or earwax irrigation; most use hearing aids. We could also learn lip reading if we weren't so blind!

◆ Most of us grew up on the edge of the fluoride revolution in dentistry, so we're still likely candidates for cavities as well as **periodontal disease**. Ninety percent of us will be affected by the latter, giving true meaning to "long in the tooth!" The best advice: brush twice daily, floss, and visit the dental hygienist at least once a year. The goal is to keep all of the teeth we can and stay pain free.

◆ **Arthritis** is what most people think of when they think of aging. Gnarled paws, inflamed knees, and massive aspirin-popping! For 17% of us, that's about it. Most people get it when they're younger and it gets progressively worse and chronic, which needn't be. Some arthritis can be stopped in its tracks if found early enough; most can be managed and permanent disabilities prevented. The form most commonly seen is rheumatoid arthritis, which appears in our 30s and 40s. Aspirin is still the wonder drug. But osteoarthritis comes from the gradual disintegration of cartilage. We get it early but feel it in our 50s. Keeping our weight down, exercising, and regular stretching are helpful. Keeping in contact with our physician makes sense here to stay current with the wonders taking place in pharmacology and genetic treatment.

◆ **Diabetes** is a major concern as we age. It's an endocrine disorder that requires strict attention to diet and lifestyle. There are two kinds. The one that is new to seniors is the maturity-onset diabetes, affecting 14 million Americans. It usually appears after 40 and is controllable, mostly by diet and exercise. The affected do not need insulin but must pay strict attention to a treatment regimen to reduce disability that generally affects the eyes and limbs. Over 80% are overweight when diagnosed. We should always get tested for diabetes at our regular exam.

◆ If diabetes isn't the greatest fear of seniors, then surely **Alzheimer's disease** is. While it's not as prevalent as we think (at the most, four million have it or a similar form of dementia), it is devastating in the loss of memory and function to the person and the violent disruption it makes in the lives of their families. It usually appears in the 60s, is psychologically devastating in its early stages, and survival is generally less than five years. There is no known cure at present.

These are the factors to consider when we establish a second life baseline with our doctor. What problems or conditions we have now, what might we expect in the future based on our family history, and what our lifestyle might inflict upon us. This proactive knowledge, with a program to confront each need as it arises, puts more control of our future in our hands.

What must we do to maintain good mental health?

Taking control of our lives may also be the single most important thing we can do to develop and maintain our own mental well-being. Being in control silences helplessness and despair, the true foes of age.

It's important to know that while we will slow down, functionally we won't be much different mentally in 30 years than we are now. We have no more reason to fear instant insanity or sudden senility than we do to expect our hands to suddenly turn green.

Senior mental health isn't an oxymoron nor do all consider aging as synonymous with mental decrepitude. In China, where age is honored, the elderly perform much higher on tests than their American counterparts.

Granted, some seniors are dithering, bewildered, and uncertain who or where they are, but most of those are very old and or very sick—and some aren't seniors at all! A third of us will function as well as ever at least into our 80s, and almost all of the rest will follow a slow, predictable path of sanity at a slower pace through our second lives.

As we read earlier, we will lose the ability to perform some mental exercises quickly. We will perform simple tasks slower, and worse if they are complex or we are surprised. (Some of that has nothing to do with the mind. We are stiffer and more afraid to do them wrong.) Our short-term memory will get poorer and we won't be able to skunk the young in such things as typing and list memorization. And in times of severe stress or major loss, we might mentally freeze up for a while. It sounds awful but we will persevere.

We'll do so because the tests that measure those dwindling capacities don't test all of the experiential knowledge and skills we gathered, including the pesky ability of older people to improvise, compensate, and unconsciously create tricks to be able to think and function just as fast (or nearly so) as our younger counterparts. Other tests show that other kinds of memory, like the procedural memory of how to play golf or swim, aren't touched by age at all.

It wasn't a total surprise, then, when a test group in Seattle, completing the same complete battery of tests every seven years, didn't steadily decline in their cognitive abilities after they passed 20. In fact, in skills that counted, they stayed about the same until they were in their 60s. Only by their 80s were there some areas of significant loss.

Who held up the best? Well educated, middle class, healthy, flexible people. The most important trait? Flexibility. In fact, Dr. K. Warner Schaie, from Penn State, who designed the Seattle Longitudinal Study, found mental flexibility—the willingness to improvise and to try unorthodox ways of doing things—a prime predictor of mental vivacity in the later years. Conversely, the more mentally rigid the person became as they aged and the lower their satisfaction with life, the quicker the deterioration of their intellect.

Schaie identified the three factors most often associated with strong mental function in older age groups to be an above-average level of education, a complex and stimulating lifestyle, and being married to a smart spouse.

Other studies show that we gain in wisdom as we accumulate life experiences and we also improve in our ability to manage our daily affairs. In fact, when tested in offering advice about fundamental matters of life, older people consistently knocked the socks off of their younger counterparts.

Our mental slippage is not due to loss of brain cells, which myth suggests die out 100,000 at a time. Rather, they remain in the brain but become senescent, or dormant, according to Harvard's Dr. Gerald Fischbach. What's more important is that there is very little loss in the cortex, where elaborate thinking takes place.

Our best hope now is two-pronged. First, we can stop this loss by helping the neurons survive. Free radicals are part of the problem, but so are stress hormones, which will do damage if elevated for too long. All of us, then, can reduce our stress.

And we can train our brain to learn again. Older brains have an astonishing ability to rejuvenate themselves, but they do it by rewiring the neurons. Studies find tutoring can recover all that was lost in the past—it was still there when retested seven years later! Even the memorization of random numbers and names. Even to prevent dementia, brain exercise and vigorous use is recommended.

Our greatest fear is that at some point we will totally lose our mental function. How would we care for ourselves or make life-sustaining decisions? Again, Dr. Mark Williams addresses this:

> For most of us this fear of becoming mentally incompetent is groundless. Much harm results from the assumption that all mental functions decline with age. We begin to believe the stereotype, which encourages us to withdraw and lose our self-esteem. Mental function does not have to decline; the capacity to learn continues through life.

Current studies of the mind and aging show four things we can do to maintain and even increase our brainpower almost as long as we live:

1. Maintain good health and a strong cardiovascular system
2. Seek intellectual enrichment
3. Exercise
4. Control our lives

Let's look at each of these to see how they might help us restructure our activities in our Great Second Life.

Good health and a strong cardiovascular system

There's no absolute correlation between a sound body and a sound mind although sickness clearly saps energy from and redirects a mind. There is a link, though, between those with heart disease, diabetes, and high blood pressure and mental decline. It's as likely to be the lifestyles that lead to both the physical and mental impairments as the diseases themselves: overeating, inactivity, and stress.

Intellectual enrichment is good for the brain

Memory loss is neither inevitable nor untreatable. Harvard neurologists are finding that later in life the brain stops producing a hormone involved in memory. So memory boosters are on the horizon: a dozen other substances are also candidates, including psychoactive drugs that could mimic the missing chemical and reinvigorate the memory.

Keeping us mentally sharp seems as simple as undertaking a variety of new, enjoyable, challenging activities. That seems to force the brain to actually grow.

Old rats provided the clue to how this happens. UC Berkeley's Dr. Marian Diamond gave toys to some rats, none to others. The neurons of the rats with the new challenge quickly sprouted new connections that enlarged the blood flow to their brains. Brains with more connections have a higher cognitive capacity. They may also resist Alzheimer's.

There were two more conclusions for humans, since the effect on rats diminished when the novelty wore off and they grew bored. So we too must vary our mental stimuli. And it won't continue if we don't "enjoy" the activity.

What might we read here? If we don't do something at least as exciting after retirement as before, we will lose ground. If we don't consciously seek something relatively new and agreeable or gratifying, we won't be keeping our mind refreshed. And if we don't plan for new and challenging activities, they probably won't happen.

Exercise gets blood to the brain

We saw earlier the benefits of exercise for the body, young or old. It logically follows that the brain, being a bodily organ, would also benefit.

Science has now proven the point. In tests, humans who exercised did better in cognition and mental performance. The exercise increased the blood supply to their brains, elevated the brain's own chemicals, and brought oxygen and antioxidants. Tests in rats showed the same result: the brains of rats that exercised increased in cognition, learning, and motor skills. Their brains were more active and in better health.

Alas, more is not better. Thirty minutes a day of walking is far better than no exercise at all. But hours of exercise in older test subjects show diminishing results.

Life satisfaction is important too

Why would liking life and being emotionally balanced be just as influential on the aging mind as mental activity? We know that those who suffer from negative emotions like depression, anxiety, and anger score lower than those who find life satisfying.

Dr. Robert Sapolsky, from Stanford, may have the answer. His theory is that the stress-related release of adrenal hormones bathes neurons in a dangerous chemical wash that can eventually damage the brain.

Knowing what's coming strengthens our mental health

An important study published in 1972 by James H. Barrett lets us see how our mental and emotional health is challenged during our second life, and what we can do to preserve our stability and confront the changes. He sees six major regressive tasks confronting the elderly:

1. accepting and adjusting to a decline in physical health, the onset of which can be delayed by a good balanced diet, regular check-ups, and exercise.
2. adjusting to a reduction in sexuality, in part related to changes in sex drive and the physical debilitation of their spouse.
3. readjustment to their dependent-independent pattern of living.
4. acceptance of a different role in the family.
5. learning to accept more than they can give.
6. reorientation to their primary social group.

Are we all subject to these six major changes? If we live long enough, probably. But an independent, well-planned life and a supportive family can delay most of them, and make the emotional transition natural and gradual.

Barrett suggests seven compensatory tasks that should help us meet these changes and make a better adjustment in old age.

The first is what this book is all about: **develop new leisure time activities to meet changing abilities and financial limitations**. We go farther on these pages by helping us identify those financial limitations, abilities, and dreams. We then try to optimally match them so that we can live the best life possible when the expenditure of that energy, ability, and funds makes the most sense.

Learn new work skills. This is particularly important to those who must or want to continue working.

The third, **readjust dietary needs**, acknowledges that we need a healthy but different diet as we age.

Adjust to changing environments recognizes that aging usually requires differing housing accommodations, often in new locales.

A hard change is to **adjust to the changing mores of society**. Every new generation has a new set of rules, music, and standards. Live and let live seems to work best here. We needn't hum rap music any more than the new set must dance the bunny hop or do the twist.

The sixth says that we must **adjust to a new status or role in society**. We're no longer top dogs; others are running the companies, community, and clubs. But we can still be vital participants and even acquire a new, different status through our new activities, if that's what we want.

The most important may be the seventh: **change your individual self-concept**. We must find a comfortable new us that will withstand the buffeting winds of a new world. We must be pleased with who we are and which of our values we want to project into our second lives. Again, by defining a Great Second Life and what is important to us, we are defining that self-concept, plus creating the ways we will live it in the years to come.

Joanne M. Schrof's article in the *U.S. News & World Report* (Nov. 28, 1994) provides excellent suggestions of what we might do at various stages of our life to stay mentally vital as we age.

◆ In childhood, eat properly (to avoid nutritional deficits that can permanently impair mental functions), get lots of stimulation (which can increase brain cell connections by as much as 25%), and stay in school.

◆ In young adulthood, make many friends, find a mentor (to get older adults' advice), marry someone smarter than you, and take adult courses (but don't cram).

◆ In middle age, develop expertise, save money (so you can afford mind-nourishing experiences), achieve your major goals then (so you don't enter retirement unfulfilled), and avoid burnout.

◆ After 65, seek new horizons, resist the temptation to settle into a comfy routine, engage the world (do things you believe make a difference in life), take a daily walk, and keep control (helplessness leads to mental apathy and deterioration).

Our biggest danger isn't loss of mental function but of just giving up, of saying "it's too late" or "why try?" This is called "disengagement," and it strikes too often shortly after retirement, when we have fewer interactions with colleagues and they are less rewarding. We're the odd person out, and the eventual result is withdrawal and isolation. It marches in hand with depression.

Its prevention and cure seem to be the same: finding and maintaining a sense of well-being, a kind of ongoing purposefulness. An examination of our lives, finding them different but acceptable. Good health also helps—plus a positive outlook and a satisfaction with life in general.

Did you ever notice that those seniors who flat-out enjoy life are having most of the fun? And there's a lot more of them around? And they live to a ripe old age? We might look for a clue there.

Planning our second life can help too. By forming a future where we build on those elements we want to share with others, we not only keep actively involved in continuously creating our own fate, it allows us to define our future role in work, our family, and our chosen social group. It's the antithesis of withdrawal.

Synchronizing our desires with our abilities

Why do we bother to do all of this? Granted, we can slow things down a bit by capping the booze and exercising—even switching from Big Macs to Little Macs. But isn't the idea to have fun in the second life, not to be forced to count calories?

You got it! To have fun; contribute again; contribute differently; find joy, then spread it to others.

Getting a handle on our health now and taking simple, straightforward steps to retain our vigor and abilities as long as possible is why we need both a baseline and a set of guidelines for future healthy living.

It also helps us better fill in our Time Box so that we realize our dreams when we have the capacity to fully enjoy and accomplish them.

What does that mean?

That if we want to hike 500 miles on the Appalachian Trail and we have an ankle tendon that's been acting up, we do three things: get the tendon tended to, train up on several shorter weekend treks, and schedule our major hike when we are young and vigorous enough to enjoy it.

Common sense? You'd think so until you talk to every other senior with plans a decade too late to perform.

It means first creating that Great Second Life health maintenance program with our physician. Determining what we must attend to immediately, what must be evaluated, how and when those treatments will take place, which chronic problems we must get under control, and how that affects our activities.

To that we add the changes we are making in our daily lives to make them healthier. And we factor in those things from our family history that may or will require attention in the future, with as many details as we and our doctor can conjure.

All of these factors are projected on a 30-year map to see in which 5-year or 10-year time pegs we will best be able to do the things we want. Some of it is absolute: we can't hike until the ankle is healed. Some is approximate: we'd like to lose ten pounds before we take part in an Elderhostel dig. Some is indeed common sense: getting our pilot's license is a sooner rather than later thing, in part because of the family's propensity to go bat blind as they age. And some is situational: we don't want to plan much for the next year because of the progressively worsening health of a terminal parent.

So we need this information for our Action Plans explained in Chapter 12.

And we need this information to lead a sensible life at any age. Since we are mortal and mortals die, we simply need it to live the best we can.

Health Sources

Barrett, James H., *Gerontological Psychology*. (Thomas, 1972).

McKhann, Guy M., and Marilyn Albert, **Keep Your Brain Young: The Complete Guide to Physical and Emotional Health and Longevity**. (Wiley, 2002).

Rosenfeld, Isadore, M.D., **Live Now Age Later: Proven Ways to Slow Down the Clock**. (Warner Books, 2000).

Rowe, John. W., M.D., and Robert L. Kahn, Ph.D., **Successful Aging: The MacArthur Foundation Study**. (Delacorte Press, 1999).

Vaillant, George E., **Aging Well: Surprising Guideposts to a Happier Life**. (Little, Brown and Co., 2002).

Wei, Jeanne, and Sue Levkoff, **Aging Well: The Complete Guide to Physical and Emotional Health**. (Wiley, 2001).

Williams, Mark E., M.D., **The American Geriatrics Society's Complete Guide to Aging and Health**. (Harmony Books, 1995). An excellent, no-nonsense guide.

For a list of aging-related health organizations (with address, phone, and website), please see the Appendix.

I have made it a rule to go to bed when there wasn't anybody left to sit up with; and I have made it a rule to get up when I have to... In the matter of diet, I have been persistent in sticking to the things which didn't agree with me until one or the other got the best of it. For thirty years I have taken coffee and bread at eight in the morning and no bite nor sup until seven-thirty in the evening... I have made it a rule never to smoke more than one cigar at a time... I smoke in bed until I have to go to sleep; I wake up in the night, sometimes once, sometimes twice, sometimes three times, and I never waste any of these opportunities to smoke... As for drinking, I have no rule about that. When the others drink, I like to help; otherwise I remain dry, by habit and preference... Since I was seven years old I have seldom taken a dose of medicine, and have still seldomer needed one... I have never taken any exercise, except sleeping and resting, and I never intend to take any. Exercise is loathsome. And it cannot be any benefit when you are tired; and I was always tired.

Mark Twain

Chapter 7

Money and Your Second Life

If the retirement financial gurus are to be believed, a chunk of our first dollar (or newborn rattle)—and every cent since—should be immediately banked so it can compound for our assuredly shaky and most likely disastrous economic future!

Their claims are mostly overblown and their predictions far too dire, but there are sensible reasons why the young should start thinking about and saving for their later years, so it isn't a heavy pecuniary burden while they are young nor are there any needs or options unmeetable when they age. Reasons too why we should get our present spending and saving under better control.

This chapter looks realistically at money and a Great Second Life. Its purpose is to help us best use our available budget to achieve the most satisfying and rewarding future. It will send us to other books listed at the end of the chapter for their expert formulae, strategies, and techniques designed to help us create the kind of savings and growth investments needed to free us up from second life financial concerns.

Here we are far more interested in what we want to do with that money. How it will help us realize our second life dreams. Otherwise, we're all madly gathering goods, instead of living now, without any idea of why we want them or what they are for.

We need to take a hard look at where our present assets are and what they amount to, plus what those might be worth in coming times. As well, we need to see how we create our income and how we spend it. And we need a flexible Money Worksheet that we can use later (and throughout our life) to see how and when we can finance our future dreams. So charts we will see—and use.

Four components of our overall financial plan deserve comment too: the basics, emergencies, how long we plan to work, and our will. Then 26 guidelines plucked from the best financial planning minds, distilled, and offered to help create a fully affordable Great Second Life.

Money is important to a Great Second Life

The old system doesn't make much sense

The conventional money approach to "getting ready for the future" or "saving up for our old age" doesn't make much sense— work like maniacs in our big-bucks years, save a bundle, retire, spend it as slowly as possible, hope to die instantly and painlessly, then leave a pile (plus our old clothes) to our kids.

What's missing from that picture? Us, humans with hearts. And real lives—but only one life per person, at least in this world, and if there's a later world all that money is irrelevant, if not a black mark.

Somewhere the purpose of life gets lost in the conventional approach. Without a larger purpose to all that working, saving, pinching, and willing, we become automatons going through the paces, ciphers adding and subtracting ciphers.

Breathtaking sunsets, hearing your first song performed, dropping a birdie on the third hole, selling buildings or bread, watching your kids (or kids' kids) hook a bluegill, and helping Habitat for Humanity roof a home—or reading, running, designing a patio, or ushering at church—all disappear unless we have a grander vision of why we are here and what the human miracle is all about.

At 40 or 50, the real issue isn't whether we have amassed enough money to live as we wish, but whether we know what we need the money for, have enough to realize our dreams (plus enough in reserve for unexpected surprises), and know how much we want left when we die.

It's drawing up a plan for the rest of our life, then matching our present and future resources to it and making it come true.

Drawing up that grander plan, mainly defining and accomplishing the dreams, is what this book is about.

Looking at the major financial concerns is the purpose of this chapter.

These pages don't tell you how to make money, save, buy stocks or bonds, invest, or even spend, although they may touch on most of those. There are scores of other books by financial experts that dwell on each topic. Here we focus on a second life plan and how money fits in.

The two are distinct. We will all have a second life, unless fate ordains otherwise. That much is free. It comes with the human territory. But we won't all have the same amount of money, and some of us will have very, very little. Wherever we are on the resources scale, a Great Second Life nonetheless involves living our latter days as fully and enjoyably as possible.

Rich or poor, we all get to look at and enjoy the same lush meadows and midday sun. We can dream, of jousting, juggling, or talking with kings. We can pray and sing and construct. We can read and write and compose. We can invent, share, and teach.

And, as noted, we all get second lives. We don't need to plan or save to have Great Second Lives, but it sure helps. The planning lets us do more things at appropriate times. And having some dispensable cash, plus some fall-back reserves, gives us many more choices.

In Part Two of this book we will design the kind of Second Life we want, and create an Action Plan broken into time-pegs so we will have a rough idea of when we will need specific inputs of money to make our dreams come true.

Here we must discuss, in broad terms, the basics we need to live a decent life: shelter, food, clothing, transportation, medical expenses, and so on. Plus an emergency contingency to weather extraordinary costs or just to dip into in hard times.

We must also look at how long we intend to create income. Will we flee the work force the moment we qualify for retirement? Fold our tent at 65? Work whenever we want spot cash? Or keep our foot in the employment camp almost forever?

And what is our post-life goal? Are we gathering it all up just so we can have it distributed (after taxes) to our children who outlive us? Or would we rather spend and distribute it before the harps start strumming?

A final thought before we look at the particulars.

There can be a strong argument in favor of "working like a maniac and saving up a bundle in our first life," if we substitute "hard" for "like a maniac." But only if that earning fervor is matched by other, equally important concerns: getting a solid education, having as many quality growth and vocational experiences as possible, building a corps of supportive friends, and creating a rich personal life. All while identifying those characteristics you want to exemplify and have associated with your name, like honesty, integrity, dependability, perseverance, and trust.

Only a minute, enlightened few have an overriding life plan when we're young. Most of us barely have a plan for next Tuesday. We're creatures of nature, as we saw in Chapter 4. We're finding out who we are and what's important. Hard work can be a valuable component of that search, and saving is a huge plus, in part because of what it says about our ability to know, prioritize, and discipline our desires. It also gives us choices later on, when our working vigor may be less. And it moves us from having to rely on fate, by putting our future as well as the present more into our own economic hands.

So if we've been working and saving and are now thinking about the coming years, we simply have more beans to count, shuffle, and spend. How many beans? Let's see.

What we have now and may have later

There's something ethereal about discussing finances without knowing what we have in the coffers. So now's the time to do a tally, then some projections so we can guesstimate where we will be at some arbitrarily critical points in our future.

First we must see what we have available in income, then what our expenditures are. From that we can create a Second Life Money Worksheet. All can be done annually or for specific time periods.

Completing each now serves as a baseline for our calculations both in Part Two of this book and to use in seeing how much separates us, financially, now from where we'd like to be at certain points in the future. Past income tax forms are helpful in making these calculations. (To produce your own forms, simply copy these or download them at the website locations indicated.)

Second Life Income Worksheet / Year or Age:

INCOME	(1)	(2)	(3)	(4)	(5)
(1) Annual / (2) Monthly / (3) Begins in Year / (4) Ends in Year / (5) Reserve					
Social Security $					
Retirement benefits					
Disability benefits					
Survivor's benefits					
Pension plans					
Employer					
Voluntary (IRA, Roth, 401[k], Keogh)					
Veteran's benefits					
Interest					
Dividends					
Early retirement bonus					
Insurance payments					
Life insurance					
Health insurance					
Long-term care insurance					
Disability insurance					
Conversion of personal investments					
Retirement savings					
General savings					
Property and goods					
Mutual funds					
Treasury bills					
Stocks					
Bonds					
Certificates					
Annuities					
Loans receivable					
Inheritances					
After-death inheritance					
Living inheritance (cash gift transfers)					

INCOME (2)	(1)	(2)	(3)	(4)	(5)
(1) Annual / (2) Monthly / (3) Begins in Year / (4) Ends in Year / (5) Reserve					
Working Income $					
Full-time employment:					
Part-time job:					
Part-time job:					
Self-employment income					
Residual income (royalties)					
In-kind income (companion, house tender)					
Home income					
Rental income					
Sale income					
Reverse mortgage					
Rental / sale of other real estate					
Gift income					
Personal holdings					
Sale of personal possessions					
Sale of collectibles					
Sale of car, boat, trailer, camper, etc.					
Other sales					
Use of emergency fund					
TOTAL INCOME $					

If this is a library book, please do not fill in this page! For a free, full-page download of this form, see www.super-second-life.com/form7A.htm

Second Life Expense Worksheet / Year or Age:

EXPENSES	(1)	(2)	(3)	(4)	(5)
(1) Annual / (2) Monthly / (3) Begins in Year / (4) Ends in Year / (5) Reserve					
House payment or rent $					
Maintenance					
Furnishing					
Improvements					
Property tax					
Food					
Utilities					
Water					
Electricity					
Gas					
Oil					
Trash / Sewage					
Other:					
Inflation (2-3% a year)					
Phone					
Computer costs					
Clothing					
Purchases					
Cleaning					
Health costs					
Care					
Medicine					
Taxes					
Federal					
State					
Local					
Self-employment					
Transportation					
Car payments					
Gas, oil, repairs					
Parking					
Commuting / public transportation					

EXPENSES (2)	(1)	(2)	(3)	(4)	(5)
(1) Annual / (2) Monthly / (3) Begins in Year / (4) Ends in Year / (5) Reserve					
Professional fees　　　$					
Gifts and donations					
Loan repayments					
Loan debts					
Personal care					
Care of family members or dependents					
Education					
Exercise / Fitness					
Travel / Vacation					
Savings investment					
Emergency fund					
Hobby costs					
Pets					
Entertainment					
Divorce costs (alimony, child support)					
Interest: credit card and other					
Assumed debts: children/others					
Insurance: Health					
Auto					
Property					
Life					
Disability					
Liability					
TOTAL EXPENSES　$					

If this is a library book, please do not fill in this page! For a free, full-page download of this form, see www.super-second-life.com/form7B.htm

Second Life Money Worksheet / Year or Age:			
Annual basic living expenses		(A)	$
Annual basic income:			
Annual Social Security income	$		
Annual pension income	$		
Other annual income: Royalties	$		
Other annual income:	$		
Other annual income:	$		
Total income (add totals above)		(B)	$
Annual basic income deficit/surplus	(A) - (B)	(C)	$
Monthly supplemental income needed	÷12	$	
Special second life expenses this year	(from Action Plan)	(D)	$
Total money desired for this year	(A) + (D)	$	
Maximum income deficit/surplus	if C is -, (C) + (D) if C is +, (C) - (D)	(E)	$
Monthly supplemental income needed	÷12	$	
Additional income source(s):	Amount		
Income source:	$		
Income source:	$		
Income source:	$		
Income source:	$		
Income source:	$		
Income source:	$		
Income source:	$		
Income source:	$		
Additional income available this year	$	(F)	
Total income deficit/surplus this year	C + F	$	

If this is a library book, please do not fill in this page! For a free, full-page download of this form, see www.super-second-life.com/form7C.htm

Second Life Net Worth Worksheet / Year or Age:					
NET WORTH	Now	1 Year	5	10	15
Assets					
Checking account(s) $					
Savings account(s)					
Bond(s)					
Certificate(s)					
Market value: home/apartment					
Market value: other real estate					
IRA and Keogh plans					
Cash value of life insurance					
Surrender value of annuities					
Equity: profit-sharing / pension					
Market value of stocks					
Market value of bonds					
Market value of mutual funds					
Current value of car(s)					
Current value of household furnishings and appliances					
Current value: furs and jewelry					
Loans receivable					
Other assets					
Total Assets (A) $					
Liabilities					
Mortgage balance $					
Loans: auto					
Loans: student					
Loans: home equity					
Current bills					
Credit-card balance					
Other debts:					
Total Liabilities (B) $					
Current Net Worth (A)-(B) $					

If this is a library book, please do not fill in this page! For a free, full-page download of this form, see www.super-second-life.com/form7D.htm

How much should we have saved?

Who knows? If we need a heart attack, simply do the calculations in most of the books cited at the end of this chapter. It's seldom under $1,000,000, often two or three times that. And if you didn't start saving at seven, you'd better clone a second you earning full income to catch up!

Don't panic. We all agree that a regular savings program begun early makes huge sense later on. That 401(k) and similar programs are super. Pensions are a blessing. Even IRAs are fine. That what might save our bacon is compounded interest, the longer to compound the better.

If we had just been as brilliant in our wild days as we are now, reading this book, we'd know why we want this windfall and it would be a lot easier to make modest sacrifices to make those future dreams come true. But we didn't, and even if we had read these words at 25, or maybe even 40, we would probably have laughed our immortal laugh and said, "Later, I'm too busy living now."

We won't starve to death. We won't have to live under bridges. But we may have to trim our dream sails to match a lesser wind.

It's never too late to lead a Great Second Life, and if our lack of savings means that we have to keep working a bit longer or settle for a trip to Tulsa instead of Tahiti, there we are. (Too humid in Tahiti anyway.) What's most important now is when we'll need special jets of money to brighten up our later days.

Great Second Life money

In Part Two we will define the dreams that will highlight our second life. Most of them cost money, so we will use the numbers in the Second Life Money Worksheet, estimate the cost of those second life dreams, and plug them all into our Action Plans.

How do we know now how much money we must save and earn to do what we want with at least some comfort and security? We don't, and we won't really know until then. For one thing, we may die first. (That's a tough way to save money.) Or what costs a dollar now may cost ten then (or 40 cents). Or we may have a vastly different concept of that dream then than now. So putting future price tags on dreams is very hard.

There's another point, too. If we don't have the funds at that time, we just won't do it, or we'll do the part of the dream we can afford, or we'll do it vicariously (which should be free). Or we may come out of "retirement" (again) and work long enough to muster up the mammon.

What's more vexing than trying to financially plan without numbers? Have patience. There's no rush. Some of these activities are 20 or 30 years away.

Emergencies

At any stage of our adult lives it is prudent to have at least six months of full earning set aside in a compounding emergency fund. That is no less important as we age.

The fund can cover a dozen calamities in our youth, and is a substitute bread winner should we become disabled, to tide us over until disability insurance or other forms of back-up support kick in. It also pays the bills between jobs, relieving the panic of having to accept any job at any rate just to feed mouths and pay rent.

But as we enter our second life, an emergency fund often meets two key needs: loss from job income and to pay non-insured medical expenses, including nursing home costs. In later years, we can also supplement Social Security income from the interest it earns.

How long do we plan to work?

When almost all work was back-breaking and only the hardy survived to 65, retirement was a blessed goal. But in today's economy, the Social Security one can earn at 65 (or a few years later as the collection year is moved up) can pay for about 40% of our needs. (For the rich, this may be as low as 25%. For those with a very modest income, it can be as much as 70%.) The age that we stop working may largely be dependent upon whether we have been able to gather the remaining percent of our current income needed to fill the gap to the 70% or so we will later require.

Add to that 70% any expensive desires in our Great Second Life plan, or any grand leap in the cost of the basics, and our choice of leaving some tangent of the work world may not be ours at all.

There are also those who simply enjoy working—it's called "play for pay." Some of us will want to be fully employed until they bronze us and put us in the hall. Others will seek part-time employment, and still others, as-needed jobs.

And how many are gnawing at the bit to leave the conventional workforce to start our own latter-life company? Or become consultants? Or work-at-home spot job independents? Or supertemps? Or authors in print?

Not included in the above are the thousands of volunteer positions, some of which have perks with economic value, like special discounts and free meals.

So when we stop working is based on many factors, not the least of which is how we see working as part of our second lives. For some of us, it will be an integral element that we will plan around. It may be the vehicle that will get us abroad, after which we will attach a month of leave to enjoy the locale. Or we may work in the summer when the tourists come calling, and go visit them the rest of the year. We may work the ski season or when the ponies are trotting or for one semester each academic year.

Employment in our second life becomes another tool of opportunity. If we keep our skills sharp and current, our teeth in, and our antennae up to job availabilities, it allows us to afford to expand the number of things we can do with the earnings.

There are some tricks to happiness in post-retirement jobs, too. One is to pick a field you love, usually one you've explored on your own (or wanted to) while you were working. Hobbies or special skills are a place to start. Then thoroughly research the job market, and if you find something, go right for it. But if there's little available, become a volunteer in the field: they are the first to hear when spots open. Finally, just be yourself, buoying your maturity and experience with a youthful enthusiasm.

Our will

How we plan this life is directly influenced by which or how many of our goods we want to—or think we should—leave behind.

Are our kids dragging out their lives until they get our inheritance? Do they grow pale at the prospect of us finally visiting Greece "on their money"? Are they living in cardboard shacks until they get the plantation? Is there an "ex" waiting to sue for the booty? Should we think about getting a direct-feed resuscitator so no one can find the plug?

Or are we hoping to spend every last dime?

If it's the latter, then Stephen Pollan and Mark Levine's book, ***Die Broke***, provides a step-by-step process so we can live this life fully while creating the needed security and income flow to make that happen.

Or we can take a modified road between leaving a bundle or nothing by cutting it as close as possible and leaving, by default, anything that's still unspent.

The **Die Broke** approach has much to commend it for any Great Second Lifer, even if leaving an intended or accidental inheritance isn't important. It is based on four key points: (1) quit our job today, (2) pay almost everything with cash, using credit only in emergency and for things that are too expensive, like homes and cars, (3) don't retire, and (4) die broke.

Quitting our job today means quitting mentally. Forget corporate loyalty—the corporations have forgotten us. Don't use our jobs to define who we are. Simply sell our services to the highest bidder, then give that lucky boss the kind of work they are paying for. Become a free agent, and always keep our eyes open. Don't confuse emotional wealth with financial wealth; that is, don't expect the job to feed us emotionally. Look for that elsewhere. Then if the job does provide emotional support, all the better.

Paying cash makes us more aware of what we're spending by slowing the whole process down. We see the actual money leaving our hands. We write ourselves one check a week for all the expenses.

Don't retire—always keep working. We'll probably need the income, we'll stay better informed, and we'll have fresh money to finance our dreams. Say Pollan and Levine, "Look at your working life as a lifelong journey up and down hills rather than a single climb up a steep cliff that ends with a fatal step off the edge (and into the abyss) at the arbitrary age of sixty-five." The idea is as much to stay active as earning: going to school, working part-time, starting a business. But always earning or learning.

And die broke. They cite four reasons why it no longer makes sense to leave inheritances: (1) Creating and maintaining an estate does damage to the person doing the hoarding—the problem of whether to spend for yourself or leave it to the kids, (2) It hurts society; the frozen investments contribute little to the productivity of the economy, (3) It hurts families because the dynamics of the relationships suffer, and (4) It hurts the recipient. It erodes their motivation and drive to work.

If we want to share our wealth with our kids, or others, why let the state dilute it through taxation? Why not just give gifts (up to the $10,000 annual tax-free maximum) when they most need it and we can most afford it?

How would Pollan and Levine have us spend our money, after meeting obligations? On experiences and education.

Die Broke gives the details and the order, including excellent advice about annuities, reverse mortgages, various forms of insurance, and serial investing (for a home, college, then retirement).

Some additional, important thoughts

Let's share some particularly appropriate second life financial guidelines, plucked from the best current financial planning books, compressed into 26 action steps, and divided into two categories: (1) income and assets and (2) expenses.

These make particular sense if you have a financial feel for where you are now and a rough notion for where you might be at key stages in the future. You can get that by completing the worksheets a few pages back—or you may wish to use the tables in Daniel Kehrer's *Kiplinger's 12 Steps to a Worry-Free Retirement* or Ralph Warner's *Get a Life: You Don't Need a Million to Retire Well*, both widely found in local libraries. See the source list at the end of this chapter.

Income and Assets

1. Plan on receiving Social Security (or the equivalent). As we said earlier, it may provide about 40% of our needs. Most seniors need from 60-75% of their pre-retirement income to live modestly in retirement. Figure 70%. Social Security will also continue to pay after we die, helping provide for our latter-life children (until 16, longer if in college), our spouse (even ex-spouses, sometimes), and dependent par-

ents. Doomsayers notwithstanding, Social Security may look a bit different but it will still be around. *Want to know how much you will receive? Call (800) 772-1213 or check www.ssa.gov/mystatement/.*

2. Most of the rest of our retirement income will probably come from our pension at work, similar programs if we are self-employed (like Keogh and SEP-IRAs), and from any IRA money we slipped out annually before filing taxes. If we lucked into some form of "golden parachute" for early retirement, that can be a big help too. For most, pensions and savings are what later provide that needed 30% of our present income for a more comfortable second life.

3. Add to that any additional savings or personal investments (like money market stocks, bonds, property, collectibles, or annuities) and we may already have more than we need to do as we wish later.

4. If we do, bingo—because the moment our second life starts that money isn't going to simply fall in our hands! We will extract it in planned portions, with the principal continuing to earn compound interest as long as it lasts, which may be long after we are using the bank eternal!

5. Not planning to retire? All the better. Any income we continue to earn once we are at the comfort stage keeps adding up and compiling more interest, which earns even more interest. We can even delay drawing Social Security for a few more years, earning an additional 8%, inflation adjusted.

6. If our folks or kin were kind enough to leave us some form of inheritance, that could proportionally increase our financial freedom. (Alas, if that kind soul had gifted it instead during their life, they would have probably saved in taxes and we could have been investing that too, compounded, to free us up even more. But we don't want to sound ungrateful.)

7. Sometimes, sadly, somebody dies and we are the beneficiary of their life insurance. But we can't depend on this—and it's imprudent to speed it up. Still, it means more funds, which means more choices.

8. While not income per se, if we have insured ourselves for disability and that occurs, that may help keep us solvent in our later years.
9. And we will have access to Medicare and Medicaid (or whatever they are called) to help offset our main health costs. Like Social Security, some sort of net will be there.
10. Most people enter their second lives with a home mortgage substantially or totally paid. (The happiest retirees are those without house payments at all. Many of them got there— and saved as much as $150,000 or more in interest—by fattening up their monthly mortgage payments. They probably paid their credit cards first, then slipped in a few extra bucks on the mortgage principal each time.) If we subtract the house payments, we also need less income. And kids gone can reduce our annual expenses as much as $15,000 each.
11. Having a low or paid mortgage can be a financial boon if we down-scale and sell the big house, which is easier to do if the kids are gone and we tell freeloaders that we have become deranged. Or we can simply live there forever and either will it to our heir(s), Pollan and Levine be damned, or we can use it as a new source of steady income through reverse mortgaging, should our health or other expenses outpace our savings—or we live far too long!
12. Another way to "find" income is to take any savings we make by not having to pay credit card interest or not having car payments and put that amount either into the bank to compound or to add it to the mortgage payment. When we make the last house payment, we might take a victory trip on what we would have had to pay the next month or two, then put the subsequent monthly non-payments into our own account. Since we're used to spending that money anyway, why not give it to ourselves to grow on our own behalf?
13. When we sell off the toys—the boat, the snowmobile, the trailer, etc.—we not only get a boost in bucks, we no longer have to pay for their upkeep, license, or storage.

14. There's another win-win that, if done right, can bring as much joy as income: if single, marry again, pool your combined retirement holdings, and cuddle into the twilight! Prenuptial agreements are in order here, even if we're Willard Scott regulars in the centenary club.

Expenses

15. The main idea in our second life is to not let our expenses get ahead of our budgeted reserves and income.
16. But life isn't always that kind; the two are seldom in perfect balance. We can't just keep making soup of our pets or lowering the winter heat. When or if it gets out of balance, we must get some advice, cut back on the excessive spending, or find some new income, like reverse mortgaging or taking on a part-time job.
17. While we won't spend nearly as much in retirement as we did before (unless we go batty), we will continue to have bills that must be paid: maybe a house payment or rent, utilities, phone, doctor, and food. Those are the core costs that our savings should meet.
18. Physical and mental health are more important than money, it's said, so if we are blessed with good health, we should spend to keep it so. If not, we must get it as good as possible, then sustain or improve it. That means that the costs for treatment, medicine, fitness or exercise, transportation, education, and some entertainment have high priority. Also long-term insurance, which should be considered and probably begun when we are young and healthy.
19. The happiest retirees are the most active, so other elements of that high quality of life might be travel, hobbies, public service, even pets. Volunteering and personal growth aren't free either, but those expenditures can be especially valuable.
20. The biggest fear of most retirees is that the moment they leave a secure job they will catch or suffer some disastrous

malady and be consigned to a full-care facility for their last 30 years! A foolish fear, numbers tell us, since the percentage of people in a nursing home at any one time is 5.2%. (Most of those spend less than a year there, often their last.) So the million-dollar reserve nest egg for that "certainty" probably costs ten times its worth in ulcers, overtime, and exhausted spouses during our prime earning years.

21. But we will have health costs, so an important budget item is insurance, then Medicare supplements, and finally personal money for co-payments, full payments, and prescriptions. This usually stabilizes and the cost is manageable. Often it goes down in the final years.

22. One expense that can put a big dent in our budget is a car. If we're used to buying a new car every 40 minutes (worse yet, leasing one), we must think twice or thrice. It's best to wait to buy until we have the cash, or get a car that's a year or two older, or keep our current clunker rolling.

23. Divorce is a real second life bummer. It can reduce a well-financed couple to two marginal survivors. One solution? Strengthen the marriage earlier so at retirement it is intact. One way to do that is to actively collaborate to make Great Second Lives a dual reality.

24. If we're still using credit cards with abandon, we've simply got to get our expenses on a tighter budget. Unless our cards have no or a low fee, the 18-24% interest can quickly undermine years of sensible saving. Reduce the cards to one, then limit its use to emergencies or for big-ticket items.

25. We may still have lingering obligations into our retirement years, like assumed debts for our kids' schooling. It's best to pay them off as soon as possible, to lower our monthly outflow.

26. The hardest financial burden is when we are entering our own second lives with dependent parents, bless them. But it may not be nearly as bad as it appears. We must sit down and figure out their income or support sources—like pen-

sions, savings, and Medicare—before assuming that their entire support will all have to come from our savings.

This information should help us better prep for a freer future. But what do we do with the four model worksheets?

We will need at least the Money Worksheet for chapters 12 and 13, "Converting Your Dreams into Action Plans" and "Can You Afford All Those Dreams?" The Net Worth Worksheet tells both where we are now and where we will be later.

We can create a worksheet for each year or for coming time-pegs, usually at the start or end of five- or ten-year time periods based on age, i.e., 60. While the basic income and expenditures may vary some annually, the key item is (E), the maximum income deficit or surplus. If a surplus, that's what we have to finance our dreams. If a deficit, attention may be needed to keep the ship afloat!

Financial or Investment Sources

Collins, Victoria F., *Your Next Fifty Years.* (Henry Holt, 1998). Solid, straightforward thinking.

Gerber, Michael E., *The E-Myth Revisited.* (HarperBusiness, 1995). If you're going to start a business, this is *must* reading.

Godin, Seth, *If You're Clueless about Retirement Planning and Want to Know More.* (Dearborn, 1997).

Hinden, Stan, *How To Retire Happy: Everything You Need to Know about the 12 Most Important Decisions You Must Make before You Retire.* (McGraw-Hill Trade, 2000).

Holzer, Bambi, two books: *Set for Life: A Financial Planning Guide.* (Wiley, 2000) and *Retire Rich: The Baby Boomer's Guide to a Secure Future.* (Wiley, 1998).

Keeffe, Carol, *How to Get What You Want in Life With the Money You Already Have.* (Little, Brown and Co., 1995).

Kehrer, Daniel, ***Kiplinger's 12 Steps to a Worry-Free Retirement***, 2nd ed., revised and updated (Random House, 1995). Has excellent charts to see where you are and what you need, though the figures are getting dated and you'd have to save millions, using their formula, to retire worry-free. Out of print, but check the library.

Lee, Dee, and Jim Flewelling, ***The Complete Idiot's Guide to Retiring Early***. (Alpha Books, 2001).

Malaspina, Margaret, ***Don't Die Broke***. Bloomberg Press, 2000.

O'Shaughnessy, Lynn, ***Retirement Bible***. (Wiley, 2001).

Patterson, Martha Priddy, ***The Working Woman's Guide to Retirement Planning: Saving and Investing Now for a Secure Future.*** (University of Pennsylvania Press, 2nd ed., 1999.

Pollan, Stephen and Mark Levine, ***Die Broke: A Radical Four-Part Financial Plan***. (HarperBusiness, 1998).

Scholen, Ken, ***Reverse Mortgages for Beginners: A Consumer Guide to Every Homeowner's Retirement Nest Egg***. (NCHEC Press, 1998). An excellent guide.

Warner, Ralph, ***Get a Life: You Don't Need a Million to Retire Well.*** (Nolo Press, 4th ed., 2002). Realistic, easy to read with interesting interviews with second lifers. Promises you won't end up a bag person, unless of course bags are your thing.

Wasik, John F., ***Retire Early—And Live the Life You Want Now: A 10-Step Plan for Re-Inventing Your Retirement***. (Owl Books, 2001).

For a list of aging-related financial or investment organizations (with address, phone, and website), please see the Appendix.

"The first forty years of life give us the text; the next thirty supply the commentary on it."

Arthur Schopenhauer

Part Two

Planning, Implementing, and Living a Great Second Life

"Middle age is when you have met so many people that every new person you meet reminds you of someone else and usually is."

Ogden Nash

Chapter 8

Dreams

It starts with a seemingly simple question, "If you had all the money, time, and energy you needed and were free from outside constraints, what would you do to put purpose and fun in your extra 30 years?"

That's the first step to an exciting future that you create!

The idea is to put on paper anything that comes to mind, however bizarre, rational, flighty, heart-pounding, mundane, spine-tingling, impractical, thought-provoking, or ephemeral.

To help, this chapter provides the reason, the tools, and the form needed to create your own dream list while it also begins a parallel feature—an example that helps guide you through the steps suggested in the chapters that follow.

Do you have a mate or playmate with whom you want to spend those future years? No problem. We will address that too, and later, in a special chapter, explain how to both blend and bend your future lives to accommodate each of your needs.

It starts with a dream. This chapter elicits dreams

Creating your own world

If you're going to create your own future world, why not do it 110%? Why not list absolutely everything that you want to do, see, experience, contribute, or know—plus more? Then build your reality around those hopes?

Will all of them come true? Probably not, if you let your hopes really soar. (Of course, if you just list one or two things, like growing old and earning less, you might bat 100%!)

Given those terms, wouldn't you rather bat less, shoot for the stars, and reach the moon?

What's stopping you? Reality? Money? A gimpy knee? What's stopping you is *you*. Nobody told you that dreaming BIG was permitted, even urged. Or you learned to expect little so there was less disappointment.

What foolishness when you're at the starting line for your last great race. So what if you come in third or 333? Every runner is a winner. Dreams are the price of participation. The losers sit on the sideline and gripe and moan and wonder where their life and all the fun went.

I'm both permitting and urging you to DREAM BIG. That's what this chapter is all about.

It starts by asking yourself, "If I could design my life from here on, what would it look like?"

Mind pictures. Word pictures. Dreams.

We know they are dreams, but we must dream anyway. Without them, without new vision, nothing happens. The next 30 years become an extension of the last 40 or 50, with wrinkles. We might make changes but they'll be done without a grander design.

You've got lots of years left to do what you want. You're smart, you've got half a lifetime of experience to draw from, you know what you like, and the sooner you get to it, the longer you will have to enjoy it.

Do you like to read? Travel? Serve on the school board? Build dog houses? Fish? Crochet? Deliver Meals on Wheels? Play with the grandkids? Write books? Coach fifth-grade soccer? Beat Free Cell on your computer? Teach? Walk across Ireland? Mentor teens? Speak to associations? Convert fixer-uppers?

The real miracle is that we get the extra 30 years! It's like being given an unlimited selection of supplies and told to build something. But we need a blueprint, and before the blueprint, we need some exciting ideas of what we want to build.

Those ideas are the dreams, and the process in this book is your blueprint. You are the builder.

What you build will be your physical, emotional, and spiritual home for the rest of your days. Lots of dreaming required.

You must make your dreams come true

Dr. Michael Gerber says it best in ***The E-Myth Revisited*** when he describes **Your Primary Aim** as "the story of your life, the script you create now. First you must write it. Then you must make it come true."

Most of us let society plan the first half of our lives. Nothing wrong with that, and sometimes we have little other choice. But there's no excuse for living the second half of our life without a strategy, then putting the steps in motion to make that strategy happen, particularly because by then we have the wisdom, skills, and usually the money to do it.

Everybody lives longer now but it takes determination, discipline, self-love, and a pinch of greatness to elevate yourself through your own design as you age.

Again, Gerber hits the target:

> Great people have a vision of their lives that they practice emulating each and every day.... The differ-

ence between great people and everyone else is that great people create their lives actively, while everyone else is created by their lives, passively waiting to see where life takes them next. The difference between the two is the difference between living fully and just existing. The difference between the two is living intentionally and living by accident.

The primer tools of later-life intentionality are dreams. Ask yourself again what seems to be a simple question, "If you had all the money, time, and energy you need and were free from outside constraints, what would you do to put purpose and fun in your extra 30 years?"

Even knowing that some of those elements may be unevenly abundant, how do you plan if you don't ask? The answers are the dreams. The strategy or life plan is how we make them come true.

Internal Brainstorming

We start by asking this broad, tough question to elicit every conceivable answer.

The idea is to put on paper anything that comes to mind, however bizarre, rational, flighty, heart-pounding, mundane, spine-tingling, impractical, thought-provoking, or ephemeral.

Begin with an open-ended list, to be added to in the days, weeks, and years that follow. Don't edit. Don't judge. Just write.

The resulting list—further defined, refined, and measured by the resources at hand—is the rough stuff from which blueprints emerge.

You're not starting with a blank page, a *tabula rasa*. If you completed the "Me Now" lists in Chapter 2 and the "In" and "Out" Lists in Chapter 4, you are aware of some of the specific things that you like about yourself and some of the areas that you want to explore to greater depth.

You also know what you don't like, or what doesn't work for you.

The hardest thing is to not limit yourself unduly by what you know of your physical and financial limitations. They must be used, at most, as very rough guidelines. You now have an overview of your health, which may suggest some physical or emotional boundaries. And your financial worksheets might suggest whether you will see the sea from the deck of the ship, rowing, or wading! Use that knowledge simply to keep your dreams within the reach of reality.

A few things are certain. The second time around you won't be catching for the Cubs or buying the Taj Mahal. Big deal! There are 100 things far more exciting and useful you can do. Start listing!

Here's a place to begin that list, in pencil please...

SECOND LIFE DREAM LIST

NAME _____ Date _____

DREAMS
1.
2.
3.
4.
5.
6.
7.
8.
9.

10.
11.
12.
13.
14.
15.
16.
17.
18.
19.
20.

If this is a library book, please do not fill in this page! For a free, full-page download of this form, see www.super-second-life.com/form8A.htm

Creating your own Second Life Dream List

Did you run out of dreams? Remember, list everything that comes to mind, however improbable, that you may want to do in the future. You can add, adjust, and delete as the future arrives.

One way to help create this list is to form a mental picture of yourself as you'd like to be at some later point, then list all of the things you are doing in that picture that you want as part of your life then.

Starter questions for your mental picture might be:

1. How do you see yourself, ideally, at 55, 60, 70, 80, ...?
2. Are you married, single, with a companion?
3. Are you still involved vocationally or professionally? How much?
4. What is your financial state? How is your health?
5. Describe your relationships. Family ties? Friends?
6. What hobbies or activities are you enjoying?
7. What's important to you?

8. What purpose are you serving?
9. What gives you the most joy?
10. Are you spiritually active?

Now, translate each picture view into specifics. For example, to #10, "Are you spiritually active?" You might put into sentence form what you could do to make your answer become a future reality, such as

1. Become a church deacon.
2. Take part in a spirituality awareness program.
3. Visit the Holy Wall (Mother Church, Vatican, etc.)
4. Pray daily.
5. Actively support the orphanage in _____, Guatemala.

Don't worry about the chronology—the order of future events or activities. Later, after you've picked out the most important dreams to pursue first, you can put those top dreams in order. Just get the future plans or ideas on paper now.

Let me share some examples from participants in my second-life" workshops to give you a few ideas of what others put on their lists. You need your own dreams, of course, but sometimes seeing what others think is important acts as a pump primer.

A COMPOSITE, BORROWED DREAM LIST

conquer my fear of flying
get a part-time winery job
set up wise investment plan
take a trip without a destination
begin volunteer work with teens
change my profession
get an MFCC license
travel to New Orleans
donate more time to charities
research my family tree
learn French
volunteer two days a week
create a circle of supportive
  friends
overcome general fears
live in South America

travel to Ireland
travel to India, see Himalayas
travel to Northern Italy
improve my photography skills
write travel articles
spend more time with friends and family
exercise
shape up my kids
certify as a water aerobics instructor
deepen my spiritual life

live in Italy
reduce my credit cards to one
achieve emotional balance
go to Europe on the QE2
buy a house
expand my real estate consulting business
become a dog custodian

*For 200 more ideas,
see the Appendix.*

An example

Often it's easier to understand and follow a process when we see others doing the same thing.

So let me create a fictitious family that is struggling with the same second life transition. They are like your neighbors or your friends from work. They may earn more or less than you, and they certainly are weirder, but about 75% of what we do everybody else does. We're driven by the same needs and we tilt at the same windmills.

Rick Benson is a bored 54, co-owner of an electronics specialty supply firm that deals almost exclusively with business and corporate clients. His partner, Ed Linden, is 20 years younger and eager to buy Rick's half of the business.

Mary Jean is Rick's wife. She is 52, and after their last child began first grade she finished college, got her teaching certificate, and now is the drama and music teacher at the local junior high school. She would like to teach for six more years to receive the maximum payment from the state retirement fund.

Rick and Mary Jean met in college. Rick left in his junior year, capable but awash academically, eager to work with his hands, a new husband needing a paycheck. He was hired by a giant firm that built airplanes. He left five years later to join the sales division of a sizable manufacturing plant. At 40, Rick began his own firm, initially to broker the purchase of specific parts for both of his earlier employers.

There are two Benson children, Melinda (now 32, married with two tots, a reluctant stay-at-home mom with a degree in nutrition), and Rick Junior (30, married for three years, the Pacific Coast regional manager of 17 hotels for a large resort chain). The Benson nest has been empty for almost a decade.

Rick wants out of the small business and selling world, but not back into mega industry. He plans to sell his half of the firm to Ed in three years. His focus now is to build the equity and long-term selling base as high as he can by that time. That sale income is his entire retirement kitty, aside from $32,000 in IRAs (now worth about $48,000). He and Ed, perhaps foolishly in retrospect, decided earlier not to create 401ks or the equivalent, so they could plow the profits back into the company.

Both have agreed to the three-year sale date. Ed will pay 40% of Rick's half of the estimated value at that time, plus 10% annually, with interest, for the remaining six years. Rick figures the initial payment will be $800,000, plus at least $200,000 a year thereafter. Rick's goal is to increase that amount by 60% in the next three years. The partners and their C.P.A have just began exploring ways that the sale might be restructured to soften the tax consequences.

Rick is becoming increasingly more excited about the extra 30 years that he plans to enjoy once he leaves the firm behind. Not having to work long days, often six days a week, will be spectacular for a while, but what will he do then?

Some things he does know. He loves Mary Jean and wants their marriage to last forever, hardly knows his grandkids, has grown a bit distant from his own children, would like to see more of the world, wants to stay comfortably solvent during retirement, enjoys golf and cycling, is eager to expand his computer graphics knowledge, wants to create an intra-family website, loves getting together socially with friends, and is fairly certain that his wife's mother, now frail and at times confused, will soon become a permanent resident in his home. (Mary Jean's father passed away years ago.) His folks are hardy, happy, and financially comfortable.

But Rick has no ideas beyond that. Oh sure, he wouldn't mind living to 100, he wants to be healthy and vigorous every day of it, and he'd like to do something different that would make a dent on society, but he has no notion what that might be. He's certain that none of this will happen in the next three years. He's going to be extra busy building up his company!

A mixed bag, Rick would say, if you asked him how he felt about creating a dream list. He's not much into dream lists. But here's what he wrote:

SAMPLE SECOND LIFE DREAM LIST

NAME: Rick Benson

DREAMS
1. Remain happily married all my life—to Mary Jean!
2. Become a SCORE volunteer.
3. Spend a weekend each year fishing and hiking with just the grandkids.
4. Visit each of my children (or have them visit) at least once a year. Invite each of them to a lunch or supper (alone or with Mary Jean) every four to six months.
5. Set up a "stock" program for the grandkids where most of each holiday and birthday gift goes into their college fund. Make it usable by the entire family. Work out the details with my CPA.
6. Take a planned, annual two-week or so vacation with Mary Jean.
7. Look into Elderhostel for short vacations.
8. Explore possible business strategy consulting—self-employment on selected days and months each year, working a maximum of 60 days annually.
9. Play 18 holes of golf with buddies, plus a 9-hole round with Mary Jean or friends, weekly.

10. Get my cycle rebuilt, add a new seat and clamp pedals; then set up a twice-a-week training regimen, with a possible weekend camp/ride each year with Rick Junior and Melinda's husband, and later the grandkids when they are able.

11. Upgrade my computer when I retire, adding the newest graphics software and hardware.

12. Take classes in advanced graphics software, and possibly hire a tutor/mentor as I progress.

13. Create an intra-family website where all can contribute to a family tree, a genealogical info log, an annual family journal (from each of the families), photos of all the members as we grow, and more as we collectively decide what we want it to contain.

14. Host and edit the family website; study other, similar websites to see how it can be better.

15 Perhaps write a memoir, to be posted on the family website.

16. Find several other couples we particularly enjoy socializing with and set up a night out once a month with all of them, maybe extending that to an occasional weekend now and then.

17. Stay in touch at least weekly with my folks; see them annually, and more often as they reach the end of their lives.

18. Become more proactive with Mary Jean's mother. Coordinate her moving in with us. Oversee her finances, as she's asked me to do. Explore the hospice program for when it is needed.

19. Find a volunteer activity once or twice a week that I would particularly enjoy. Check the city volunteer organization. Ask friends.

20. Investigate running for a position on the Airport Board. Speak to the present members.

21. Dust off the clarinet? See if I can play at all? Take some refresher lessons? Join the junior college community band?

22. What can I do that will make a permanent, positive dent in our town? Ask others. See where the biggest short- and intermediate-term needs are.

23. Have a date night a week with Mary Jean.

If you have a spouse or partner?

Congratulations! They are people too, entitled to their own hopes and dreams. They also need to create their own dream lists.

Why? Because you may not reach a ripe old age (or any old age) together and they will have to fend and grow without you, hard as that may be to imagine. Or you may not reach old age mated. Or you may find yourselves still mated but drifting into separate worlds. So everybody should know what he or she wants to do with their own extra 30 years...

In that enlightened spirit, Rick asked his wife Mary Jean to create her own list, without consulting his list first.

What will they do with their lists? Later they will compare them, and perhaps add or subtract a bit from each list, influenced by the new ideas the other proposed. Let's devote Chapter 10 to what mates or spouses do together and alone with their lists.

But while we're focusing on the Bensons, this might be a good time to see what Mary Jean did put on her dream list:

ANOTHER SECOND LIFE DREAM LIST

NAME: Mary Jean Benson

DREAMS
1. Set some time aside each day to be with Rick.
2. Retire at 58 , unless I get a "parachute" offer equal in retirement income earlier.
3. Check into acting with the junior college and/or the community theater.

4. Take over the choir directorship from Madge when she retires.

5. Join the Philharmonic chorus.

6. Sing with the j.c. chorus for *The Messiah* presentation each winter.

7. Redo the landscaping and keep up the outside of the house myself, in part for exercise.

8. Get closer to the kids, and stay active with the grandchildren.

9. Teach piano to the grandchildren, if they are interested.

10. Look into getting the grandchildren full electronic keyboards, if they want to learn piano.

11. Visit England, France, Norway, Portugal, Spain, and Australia with Rick.

12. Get directly involved with hospice; also join the Board and help with the funding.

13. Spend an afternoon or day each week with my lady friends.

14. Get season tickets to the repertory and community theaters for Rick and me.

15. Buy a DVD and develop a good collection of classical, musical, and Hallmark discs.

16. Learn ballet and tap. Classes or a teacher. Maybe try out for older dance parts in musicals.

17. Write a junior high drama textbook with Lillian McCumbers. Check electronic publishing.

18. Go walking daily, swim twice a week, and play golf with Rick and the kids.

19. Get Mom set up here so she is independent but "supervised."

20. Upgrade the inside of the house; make it warmer, cozier; paint the upstairs, new toilets.

21. Mentor three drama/music kids a year as they enter or are in high school.

22. Speak to the grade school classes about great musicians; integrate music, visuals.

23. Get to know Rick's parents better.

Enough reading. Fill in Your Second Life Dream List! We need it for the chapters to come…

"For most men there should come a time of shifting harness, of lightening the load one way and adjusting it for greater effectiveness in another. That is the time for the second career, time for the old dog to perform new tricks. The new career may bring in little money; it may be concerned only with good works. On the other hand, it may bring in much needed support. It can be a delight to a man who comes at last to a well-earned job instead of a well-earned rest.

Dr. Wilder Penfield

Chapter 9

Commitment and Timing

There are some very important steps between creating a list of dreams and making them come true.

The first of those steps is deciding which of those dreams you so want to come true that you will do whatever it takes to make them happen.

The second is deciding when—the order and the actual time— you want to realize them. Not every dream can come first nor do all work at any age. Few soccer stars began at 80.

Incidentally, some dreams you may want to start tomorrow, to get a kick start now so you'll have the instructional or experiential background to excel later.

Determine your commitment, then figure out the best order

COMMITMENT

Some dreams are just dreams

It's one thing to have a dream, another to so want that dream to come true that you will commit all of your energy and skill to make it happen.

Many future dreams have a "wow!" element to them. A "wouldn't that be great if..." component. Somewhere between mild enthusiasm and the bonanza incredulity of winning the lottery—but they are short on a doing commitment. If they happen, wow! But not enough belief that they will, or real joy that they might, to muster up much hard work or close planning.

Other dreams are firmer. "My destiny" dreams fall in this category. They are the culmination of all you've read, done, or wanted. If achieved, they are your destiny realized.

So there are levels of dreams, and there are degrees of how hard we are willing to do whatever it takes, or anything, to convert them into full-fleshed reality.

Levels of commitment

The question is how we measure commitment, particularly of something projected into the future.

The percentage approach is one form of measurement, but suspect.

"I want you to play 100% today!" is the classic call to action—and every coach's desire. 100% is clear enough, but what is 98%? In baseball, is that throwing 2% slower? And what does 93% mean? Pitching with 7% less accuracy? Or moving our hands an inch up the bat? What if we wanted to play 100% but our skills only lifted us to 84%? And what if we only cared 75% but, despite ourselves, we rose to 93% in performance?

I think what we really need to provide a tough core of a Great Second Life plan is a cluster of no-holds-barred convictions. A cluster that is scattered throughout the years, like the guiding stepping-stones in a garden full of beauty.

That's why I like Dr. Robert Wubbolding's definition of commitment from his book ***Evaluation: The Cornerstone in the Practice of Reality Therapy*** (1990). He says there are five levels of commitment:

Level 1. I don't want to and you can't make me.
Level 2. I want the results but I don't want to put in the effort.
Level 3. I'll try. I might. I could.

Level 4. I'll do the best I can (with what I currently know).
Level 5. I'll do whatever it takes (including what I don't know).

In this book we are interested in number five. How does it differ from the first four?

It's almost the reverse of the first, which is a youngster's way of saying "No!" Teens use it too, without the confrontational terminology. They just dig in and do nothing, as did many of the viceroys to the King of Spain's colonial decrees, declaring *"Obedezco pero no cumplo,"* meaning "I obey but I don't comply." It's not the absence of a commitment, rather the resolve to achieve the reverse: "I won't do it!" rather than "A team of horses (or horse traders) couldn't stop me from making this happen!"

How many of us apply the second to our resolve to exercise? We would love to have the results—without the sweat! Like planning to become rich if some unknown person would leave us a fortune in their will. Not much proaction there to plan around.

And the third—"I'll try. I might, I could"—is about as lukewarm as a commitment can be. About as resounding as "I think I'll do that someday." In other words, no real commitment at all. If, by some miracle, it should occur, fine. But it's better relegated to our wish list. Too weak for our use here.

"I'll do the best I can..." is the most insidious. The fourth commitment sounds good but one's "very best" always falls short of fulfillment. What makes it dangerous is that the pledge contains the winds of conviction and the breath of potential—but at heart it's just hot air.

Still, that pledge might someday find the wings to rise above that hot air, plus the backbone to become a number five. These pledges should be written down and kept visible, on the very long shot that they may ultimately win true commitment.

Top commitment

The only kind of commitment that really counts is #5—"I'll do whatever it takes (including what I don't know)." Those are the kind of commitments we need to build a Great Second Life. They are the bricks of our new house.

Alas, even saying and believing them sometimes won't be enough. We may have a ton of intent, all the skill and money necessary, and every ingredient for success at hand but some of them may still never happen. Some of the explanations are understandable: we died first, a tornado carried away our tools, our helpmate took a powder... Or there is no explanation. Despite the desire and conviction, some will still just be words.

But the good news is that in the fifth and highest category that is the rare exception rather than the rule.

So that's our next step. Fill in our dream list as completely as we can, then look hard at each item and assign it a commitment number.

Then take a clean sheet of paper and recopy all of the #5s on it. (Put the original list in a file or drawer, to be added to and reviewed later.)

How many rose to the top? Three? Five? Ten?

"Slim pickings," we say to ourselves. Not much to build 30 years around!

We're not thinking clearly. That's plenty to get started.

Those will be the peaks of our future life. And we're still new at this dream stuff. We might double or triple that number when we get good at it. Right now it's a novelty, a sort of paper game, mostly done because I asked you to.

It will get serious when those few peaks start to take real form and we see our lives changing along with them.

And those starter commitments will expand. A major life change will necessitate smaller changes. One peak will create a chain of foothills, and soon our future will become an exciting panorama of #5 commitments. The paper game will become a life game. In a moment we will see which commitment Rick wrote on his new paper. Which of his 23 original dreams he will now "do whatever it takes!" to build a second life around.

A quick aside might be helpful here, although it is so obvious you might wonder why it is mentioned at all.

Our future life will be like the years we have already known in at least one major way: most of it will be taken up with the exigencies of just living. Things like eating, sleeping, getting from here to there, communicating, bathing, and so on. There may be less "working," in the 8-5 sense, but we may find ourselves still plenty busy doing the basics.

Much of the success of our second life will be the skill with which we integrate our new activity or commitment peaks into our basic living. And while we may work less, in the vocational sense, we may find ourselves even busier with a half-dozen new summits, and overwhelmed, at least in the beginning, if we try to initially build extensive mountain chains. So three or five or ten #5 commitments, while perhaps disappointing quantitatively, might be plenty, at least for now.

TIMING

Sometimes our dream lists look like a barnyard of second life hopes, as unlike as Herefords, hens, and horseflies. They have different ages too.

That is, some are appropriate for mid-summer chickens, others just fine for last-leg roosters.

If scaling the ten tallest Rockies is your wildest second life dream, great! But good luck if you're 97 and grappling with 400-400 vision! Mountain climbing is an early-bird dream, when (if ever) you have the strength, legs, desire, and deep-reach reserve.

Believe me. I climbed to the top of Half Dome, in California's breathtaking Yosemite Park, with my younger daughter when I was 57. We had discussed it for nearly a year, so we dressed appropriately, brought plenty of water, and planned to spend enough time at the top to thoroughly absorb the spectacular view. It took us about 14 hours, literally from dawn to dusk, to complete the 17-mile, 4900-foot trek.

Kim was in her 20s then so she still had 50+ years to repeat the venture. But I didn't, and as I write this book I'm fully aware that my vertical hiking days are drawing to a close. I think I could do it again right now, at 65, but in five or ten years I'm not sure I'd want to even if I could.

On the other hand, reading to your grandchildren (or children or great-great grandchildren) is a delight at any time. And if you aren't blessed with grandchildren, there are millions of somebody else's who would love to sit on your lap or at your feet to hear about *The Little Engine That Could.*

The lesson is clear. Put your dreams that have temporal limits in an achievable order, and let the others without time restraints fall whenever they comfortably fit.

There is another reality too. We have learned that to do well something that is important takes time and close attention. Thus setting off on two significant adventures simultaneously almost certainly guarantees that we will reach neither destination.

So the second task of this chapter is to suggest that we look hard at each of the dreams that made our top-commitment list and we subject them to serious time listing.

That means two things.

First, what is the best age for us to enjoy that commitment, given that we may have 30 or so good second life years to get pleasure from the dream? Some may be appropriate at any time. Some, like mountain climbing, are probably most fully enjoyed early on.

Then, if we have several dreams that are good starters, we might put them in priority order, selecting one to begin with, then another...

That may mean simply putting numbers in front of the top commitment dreams on our list to indicate which will be pursued in what order, keeping in mind that we can add or subtract from that list whenever we wish and we can switch the numbers at will.

Or we might want to create a Time Box where we divide the 30+ years into boxes of 5-10 years each. In the appropriate boxes we put the dreams when we want to first enjoy them.

How might that look?

TIME BOX

55-60:	60-65:
65-70:	70-75:
75-80:	80+:

Whatever form we use, if we don't list them with a starting date we run the danger of either forgetting about them altogether or deciding to play the game after that team has left the field!

Can we dabble with more than one dream simultaneously? It's our list and our life; we can do whatever we wish. We can even try them all at once. But it does make some sense to put our primary focus on one dream until we have it well launched, then move to another.

The example again!

Of the 26 activities (or dreams) that Rick initially listed, he put 11 into his "must do" category. Not that he didn't want the rest, but some were further down the tree of importance, some depended upon one or several of the eleven to take place first, and most of the rest he figured might happen on their own without undue effort or attention now.

In his mind Rick bunched the #5 choices into topic fields.

These are Rick's priorities for when the company sells (in three years) and he begins his "second life":

Rick's #5 Commitments

MARY JEAN

1.	Remain happily married all my life—to Mary Jean!
6.	Take a planned, annual two-week or so vacation with Mary Jean.
23.	Have a date night a week with Mary Jean.

FAMILY

4.	Visit each of my children (or have them visit) at least once a year. Invite each of them to a lunch or supper (alone or with Mary Jean) every four to six months.
18.	Become more proactive with Mary Jean's mother. Coordinate her moving in with us. Oversee her finances, as she's asked me to do. Explore the hospice program for when it is needed.

FAMILY WEBSITE

13.	Create an intra-family website where we all can contribute to a family tree, a genealogical info log, an annual family journal (from each of the families), photos of all the members as we grow, and more as we collectively decide what we want it to contain.
14.	Host and edit the family website; study other, similar websites to see how it can be better.
15.	Perhaps write a memoir, to be posted on the family website.

GRAPHICS

11.	Upgrade my computer when I retire, adding the newest graphics software and hardware.
12.	Take classes in advanced graphics software, and possibly hire a tutor/mentor as I progress.

BUSINESS

8.	Explore possible business strategy consulting— self-employment on selected days and months each year, working a maximum of 60 days annually.

We'll return to these in a moment, but Rick was quite surprised to see that none of his original 23 received a #1 or #2 rating. He explained that quite simply: he had probably discarded them mentally when drawing up the list. He had spent his vocational life writing lists and knew better than to waste time on what he couldn't do.

I mention this only because others (myself included) tend to think in the reverse: the wilder and least doable, the quicker it makes my list, while anything that is an extension of what I'm already doing might not get there at all. Only on longer reflection do the impossible items get bumped—usually to a #4!

Which means that both Rick and I probably need to revise our dream lists repeatedly, and leave open the possibility that at any time new ideas or dreams should be entertained—and if sufficiently desired, put on the #5 fast track. Rick because he is so cautious and conservative, me to temper my enthusiasm a bit and make room later for the obvious.

Which of Rick's dreams fell into the #3 category?

2.	Become a SCORE volunteer.
19.	Find a volunteer activity once or twice a week that I would particularly enjoy. Check the city volunteer organization. Ask friends.
20.	Investigate running for a position on the Airport Board. Speak to present members.

Did he know why they ranked so low?

"It's too early right now to see if they will still hold my interest. I've got three hard years of work ahead of me before Ed buys the company. I guess I'm just exhausted thinking about those three years. I'll look at them more seriously when I'm unencumbered."

Rick then decided to reclassify them to #4s so they would be visible to reconsider later.

All the rest were #4s, meaning not enough power right now to invest the needed energy but strong candidates when he was 57, or later.

An apparent question almost asks itself here. Does that mean, for example, that Rick won't spend a weekend a year fishing and hiking with the grandkids or that he won't stay in touch with his folks?

Not at all. He might wind up doing every one of the #4 commitments. But usually as spin-offs or lesser activities at the outset until they lift themselves up to the #5 things he wants to dedicate himself to on a regular, high-priority basis.

Isn't that unduly confusing? A well-lived second life has lots of room for fuzzy fun. Who cares if what you are doing is a #4 or #5?

Then why bother in the first place? So the bedrock things you want to do in your gift years get the attention they deserve. So that the legitimate #5 selections, the "I'll do whatever it takes (including what I don't know)" dreams, happen and infuse those last 30 years with as much productivity and enjoyment as possible.

Rick's Timing

When Rick looked at the eleven items he could see none that was particularly aged-related, though some clearly had to be done soon and others had to wait until the firm was sold and he had free time.

So he dropped the original dream list numbers and rewrote them in this priority order:

Rick's #5 Commitments

1.	Become more proactive with Mary Jean's mother. Coordinate her moving in with us. Oversee her finances, as she's asked me to do. Explore the hospice program for when it is needed.
2.	Have a date night a week with Mary Jean.
3.	Take a planned, annual two-week or so vacation with Mary Jean.
4.	Visit each of my children (or have them visit) at least once a year. Invite each of them to a lunch or supper (alone or with Mary Jean) every four to six months.

5.	Create an intra-family website where all can contribute to a family tree, a genealogical info log, an annual family journal (from each of the families), photos of all the members as we grow, and more as we collectively decide what we want it to contain.
6.	Host and edit the family website; study other, similar websites to see how it can be better.
7.	Perhaps write a memoir, to be posted on the family website.
8.	Upgrade my computer when I retire, adding the newest graphics software and hardware.
9.	Take classes in advanced graphics software, and possibly hire a tutor/mentor as I progress.
10.	Explore possible business strategy consulting— self-employment on selected days and months each year, working a maximum of 60 days annually.
11.	Remain happily married all my life—to Mary Jean!

Being more proactive with Mary Jean's mother, the first dream, couldn't wait three years. He would get to it within the next two weeks, and have it fully in motion in two months. With luck, it would be a long-term challenge and would have to be integrated into his early "retirement" years. He was grateful that this second-life planning had made this issue so prominent.

There was no reason why he couldn't do the second and third dreams right now, and continue them far into the future.

He had been so preoccupied with the company's future that their social life had indeed suffered. Recently they spent far too little quality, personal time together, so this would also be a top priority right now. They would sit down this weekend and lay out a plan to pick the night, determine who should plan the activity, and devise whatever safeguards were necessary to keep this idea alive, fun, and a permanent future event.

That begged the last item on Rick's priority, there only because he didn't know how to rank it. A happy marriage was equally important to both of them, and both wanted to grow old together. But it was more an assumption than a dream, and the reason he was eager to begin a date night each week and a planned, two-week vacation with Mary Jean right away.

Vacations had become spotty and indefinite the past few years, often trips to the home of a family member, where Rick was swept away to play golf or fish while Mary Jean focused on the children and wound up cooking and shopping. They spent less time together on the road than they did at home. But that would change as of right now.

Rick made a decision that if he was going to put in three no-nonsense years in the firm, it wouldn't be at any cost. He would simply insist on a free night a week and two weeks or more a year with Mary Jean, a safe distance from the shop. In fact, they would also plan the first vacation this weekend, he would write it in the company calendar in ink, and he would do the same the coming two years. That was non-negotiable.

The fourth item had also fallen into decline, and Rick longed for more contact with his kids. But he couldn't just dictate that they would make themselves available, so this item would take more attention and probably Mary Jean's motherly intervention or compromise. He would discuss it in the coming weeks or months with his wife, then Melinda and Rick Junior, and by this time next year, if not a lot sooner, they would set up some sort of loose, mutually-desired system of get-togethers that could easily continue into his dotage.

The next three, all related to the intra-family website, might be a common meeting ground with the kids since both were computer literate and liked the website idea. He may not have much time to devote to it until the firm was sold, but there were some things they could do in the meantime. The order was probably right; of the three, the memoir most intrigued Rick but it was the farthest away in terms of having the time to do it right.

Numbers eight and nine were definitely post-sale. Rick was fascinated by computer graphics, and could easily see himself inextricably drawn into the topic if he began too soon. So he would gather whatever he saw in print and create a starter file, then assemble the software and take the classes once the company was gone and he had the time to do so fully.

And number 10, right now he was limited to seeing what others were doing in his field, who was consulting, the current rates they were charging, and where he might have some special niche insights. He planned to begin consulting part-time well after the dust of the company sale had settled and when he was eager again to get back into his vocational field.

How might Rick's top-priority dreams look in a Time Box?

"Peculiar—and shallow," he says, laughing. "I'm so bogged down with the company's sale that I'm only thinking clearly a decade out. I'll fill in the rest once I survive the next three years!"

For now, then, Rick's Time Box might look like this:

RICK's TIME BOX

Now:	1 Year:
Attending to Mary Jean's mother Date night weekly with M.J. Planned, annual two-week vacation with M.J. A life-long, happy marriage	Schedule more time with my kids
After the company's sale:	**4-10 years:**
Intra-family website Upgrade my computer with graphics software; take graphics classes	Write a memoir Part-time consulting

Rick's presumption is that dreams once begun will continue into later-life time periods or boxes, unless mortality (in the case of Mary Jean's mother) intercedes or the dream runs its course and interest simply wanes. His list tells him when he wants to start each of the top-priority dreams this coming decade. It serves both as a memory prod and a goal to launch each dream.

"Life is a fatal adventure. It can only have one end. So why not make it as far ranging and free as possible?"

Alexander Eliot

Chapter 10

Getting in Sync With Your Mate

*It's a double blessing having a partner, companion, or mate
with whom you share your future.*

There's the companionship, of course—maybe even love!

*And there's the planning, which can be the source of great fun
and mutual accomplishment. It can also be a challenge!*

*Our task in this chapter is to remove the negative aspects of
that challenge by clearly identifying which dreams are singular and belong overwhelmingly to the dreamers and
which either overlap with the other person or are wholly
shared with them.*

*We also share a simple conflict resolution process that works
particularly well with couples, should that future planning
lead to a tug of war. This helps stop that from ever happening.*

*Something else important happens when you start comparing
and merging shared dreams—you get to really talk with
your mate about things that matter. Life-creating and life-
confirming things.*

Making sense for mated dreams and dreamers

Independence and Interrelatedness

Many reading these pages are married or have a partner and intend to keep it that way forever.

But if that isn't so—if you are single or you really don't want to spend your future with this mate (or any)—why not quickly skim this chapter anyway, just to see what it says? (Then if it becomes more applicable later, come on back!)

The idea here is to see how we can take both our own dreams and our partner's and create an extraordinary, shared second life where we each enjoy our own independence plus a special mated togetherness.

It's fairly straightforward putting our own lives in order, and though it takes some work, it's not much harder to create from it a personal future life plan that is full of purpose and fun.

It's not twice as hard to do for two—it's probably five times harder!

Why? Because by the time we've reached 45, 50, or 60, we're usually on very different tracks. Getting those tracks intentionally heading the same way, and putting exciting and worthwhile stops along them for years to come, takes energy, compromise, tact, and imagination. Huge dollops of humor also help grease the way.

A hundred years ago there was no traditional way to plan a long, happy future. People lived to 48, on an average. The nest was barely empty before the final curtain.

But 50 years ago it was far different. When one thought of making plans for the future at, say 50, the man was already about as high up as he would go at work, with his vocational future short. Most men at this point were looking for ways to ease into retirement, or perhaps toward a new, part-time job. They were dreaming of slowing down and getting caught up on fishing, golf, their other hobbies, or travel—or all four! That pattern is still widespread.

The traditional counterpart found his wife at the end of her child-raising years, with the "empty nest" already a reality or clearly in sight. The house was getting larger, the everydayness of home duties was becoming increasingly more maddening, and she was often dreaming of "making something of herself," sometimes in the very same business world her husband was gladly abandoning!

That model has changed so much in the past 20 to 30 years that the two stereotypical models now have twenty (or 120) variations. Stay-at-home pops, Fortune 500 moms, single-parent families, nannies and after-school child care in homes with two full-working parents, same-sex bondings (sometimes with kids), grandparents raising their kids' kids…

But the need to get two tracks running parallel into one hasn't changed a whit. At a certain age, mates must look to the future and decide where they want to be, as individuals and as a couple.

Or not. Or they can just let the future write the script. (The only problem with that is the future doesn't care. It just happens. Humans can take control and create the kind of days they want to spend!)

For several years now I have offered second-life planning workshops for couples, usually at association conventions, where we do lots of shared talking, then some very useful exercises, which I'll describe later in this chapter. We even discuss an easy-to-apply tool for conflict resolution.

What have been the men's primary future concerns at those gatherings? Money always leads the list. Having something to do and dreading possible debilitating illnesses come up in different guises. Only the bravest will mention three other concerns that more will admit on paper: how are they going to get along with their mate in this new role, how will they find and keep male friends now when their work contact is gone, and how will they continue to do their "manly tasks" when debility takes over?

Other than some trips and a golf or tennis match once a week, most man have no plans for two years out, after retirement. Nor anything for the remaining 20 or 30 years!

Women are far more frank about the prospect of 20-30 years or more of conjugal togetherness! Their first question? What are they going to do with him under foot 24 hours a day, expecting, of all things, that she cook his lunch?

They are equally as concerned about the finances. But they seldom worry about being busy nor do they seem overly concerned about health.

In fact, most of the women have a long list of things they want to do, enough to fill a lifetime. One of those things often involves them getting into the work force full time. Or if they are there already, adding a few more years to put a decent capstone on their own career.

When I ask if the couples have actually sat down and done any serious short- and long-term future life planning, a pall of embarrassment reigns. And if they say yes, that plan almost always means two trips and one major home repair.

When I have the gall to ask why they haven't had this crucial conversation, we hear some hard truths.

"It's pretty tough because I know we're going to disagree. It's just better to let it work itself out."

"If I open this can of worms, I know he (or she) will dictate precisely what we will do. And since it won't make much sense and I don't want to do most of that anyway, why create problems?"

"The two of us together for 30 more years? I have to think about that…"

"We never heard of anybody really planning like that. We all know that only a small part of it will happen. There will always be something to interfere."

"Why bother? We'll probably both be dead by the time we actually do any of it."

"That's why we're here, for you to do it for us."

What I hear is fear, avoidance of confrontation, inertia, or ennui. And what I suspect is that because their parents (or grandparents, whose model we more often follow) didn't do this, isn't it presumptuous of us to do—then admit it publicly? And what kind of shame would we face if we didn't follow through?

And twice I've heard that if God (or the gods) want us to have a happy future, they will make it so.

My own suspicion is that most couples are exhausted when it comes time to plan what can be the most exciting and rewarding years of their lives. They've just survived life's expectations—school, degrees, a job, marriage, kids, a home, raising the kids, keeping food on the table, braces, college tuitions... Not much latitude there, and not a whole lot of independent planning either.

Then the expectations suddenly stop. Hit 50 or so and we're in a newfoundland. Nobody lived this long and still had 30 more years to make sense of. We got the gift, but no instructions!

Then let's create some instructions so we and our spouse or mate can use the gift fully.

Let's think of a three-party contract. One party is you. The second is your mate. And the third party is both of you as a loving unit.

How can we plot 30 years that gives each of the three parties its full due? (You say that you're only going to live ten more years? Then plot ten years for you and ten together; your mate must take care of their remaining 20. Just plot faster.)

The dream list is the perfect tool.

In Chapter 8 you wrote out your dream list. Those were things you want to do in or with your remaining years. Your mate did the same.

In Chapter 9 we sprinkled a bit of preference on the list, forcing you to pick out those dreams that you really cared about and were willing to go the extra mile to make happen. Then we put the top priority dreams in some temporal order. Your mate did too.

Now we have the core of two-thirds of our future life plan on paper. How do we devise the shared part, the us as a living unit, without all of the fears and reluctance?

If you were at my workshop, after having explained the whole concept and orally synthesized Part One of this book, I would divide the group by sex (or at least kept the mates apart) while the individual dream lists were written up. The reason is simple but very important: I want each person to make their list without the suggestions, interference, or even the presence of their mate. It only works if this is *their* list and contains the things *they* want to do (if they had all the money, energy, and time, etc.).

If there's time, I would let that segregated group read their individual lists to each other, in case something else is suggested that they hadn't considered or a wish is phrased differently so the listener might hear a better way to express that dream.

I would then tell the groups to pick out the top five things on their individual dream lists that they most want to do and put those five in the order they want to do them. (There isn't time there to do all of the commitment and timing considerations in Chapter 9. They can do that later.)

When we reunite the sexes (or groups) I would remind them all again why this future planning is not only unique, it is very important. And what they are about to do as couples is the foundation for a series of talks between themselves from which will come the rarest of gifts: 30 special years unknown to their ancestors and only dreamed about by their grandparents, years they design to be lived as they wish.

I would tell you that in a moment I'm going to ask the mates to join and work together. Their task is to exchange their dream lists. I want each person to see what is important to their mate. Criticism isn't permitted—nor is heinous laughter. But they can ask for clarification and expansion on the items listed.

That reunion of the two often produces a magic moment. Too often for the first time the mate sees what their partner thinks is important and how they want to spend their coming days (and nights). What is equally surprising is how many dreams they share in common! I would allow as much time as I can for you to talk with each other about the lists, and to expand in particular about what the five top items on each list really mean.

Then would I ask each couple to take out a clean sheet of paper and to divide their lists into three columns on the new page. Let's call it OUR FUTURE LIFE PLAN.

First I would ask them to extract the dreams they share in common, decide on an accepted phraseology (since both have usually said the same basic thing differently), and list those under SHARED DREAMS. If either had numbered those on their list, move the numbered items to the top.

The two remaining columns are for the remaining items on each of the dream lists, with the top priority items first. Put at the top of the columns (MY) DREAMS and (YOUR) DREAMS, obviously inserting the proper names inside the parentheses.

What results is what others have also called their "freedom list." It is a commitment to share the responsibilities for, and the joy from, the items under SHARED DREAMS. And the freedom to do the things on your own dream list, with the tacit approval of your mate, who in exchange receives your tacit approval to do what is on their dream list. (Alas, not everything may be approved, but that too you will work out as you perfect and add to your lists. Poisoning the in-laws or a daily run to the Post Office in the nude are examples that may fall short of even tacit approval.)

What do you have in OUR FUTURE LIFE PLAN?

(1) You both have a general blueprint for the future.

(2) It can be modified, expanded, pruned, and rewritten regularly.

(3) Changes should be made with the support and approval of the mate, so both are aware of the current blueprint or plan at all times.

(4) What remains is to do the reordering of the dreams by commitment level and timing.

(5) Finally, an action plan will be developed for each shared dream, with you and your mate deciding who will create the action plan.

(6) It is up to each mate to create the action plans for their individual dreams, and to rerank them by commitment and time priority, if not already done.

How might the form look for OUR FUTURE LIFE PLAN?

SHARED DREAMS　　*/*　　Date:

_____ **DREAMS**	_____ **DREAMS**

If this is a library book, please do not fill in this page! For a free, full-page download of this form, see www.super-second-life.com/form10A.htm

What goes in which box?

How do we determine which dreams go into which box?

No brain surgery here. What is clearly your dream and comes from your dream list goes in one of the two lower sections. What is clearly your mate's dream goes in the other.

And what appears on both your dream lists, once converted into the same wording, and is something you want to share together, goes in the SHARED DREAMS section.

But sometimes what goes where isn't all that clear. Like when mates will both be doing the same thing but the action is peculiar to each. For example, if both are cigar box jugglers and wish to continue that perilous and eccentric discipline into their rigidity, the issue is whether they (1) juggle as a team, (2) both participate in the same large juggling group, or (3) juggle separately, he with Field's Flying Objects and she with the Dainty Old Ladies Who Throw Things.

The first case is clearly shared. The third is purposely singular, or personal. But I have no idea about the second item. Alas, you are mates: talk and figure it out, then list appropriately. There are no iron-clad rules. It's your plan!

Your assignment now in this chapter is to complete the OUR FUTURE LIFE PLAN form. Do it in pencil at first until you are both satisfied that it is the best you can do now. But please do it. If you don't, there's nothing to change or build from!

The Example

Let's see how Rick and Mary Jean fared when they compared their earlier plans and separated out the dreams they shared.

Unlike at a workshop where one is listing their dreams for the first time and usually has insufficient time to properly extract the top (#5) commitments, then put them in time order, both Rick and his wife have had an opportunity to spend much more time on their lists. So what we see are Rick's top commitments, in order, again, and Mary Jean's final list for the first time, both redistributed into the OUR FUTURE LIFE PLAN format.

SHARED BENSON DREAMS / Date:
Remain happily married to each other for life, and should marital difficulties occur, seek assistance at once. Set aside a minimum of 30 minutes each day for one-on-one conversation.
Become immediately more proactive with MJ's mother. Coordinate her moving in with us. MJ will design the living arrangements and conditions; R will oversee her finances and will set up the hospice program for when it is needed.
Have a scheduled weekly date with each other.
Take a planned, annual two-week or so vacation together. If possible, include England, France, Norway, Australia, and New Zealand.
Integrate R's parents more into our life. Help the children get to know them better.
Get annual tickets to the repertory and community theaters, attend the presentations.
Both take active parts in the hospice program: the Board, funding, coordinated musical visits.

RICK'S DREAMS	MARY JEAN'S DREAMS
Visit each of my children (or have them visit) at least once a year. Invite each of them to a lunch or supper (alone or with Mary Jean) every four to six months.	Join the Philharmonic chorus.
Create an intra-family website where all can contribute to a family tree, a genealogical info log, an annual family journal (from each of the families), photos of all the members as we grow, and more as we collectively decide what we want it to contain.	Sing with the j.c. chorus for *The Messiah* presentation each winter.

Host and edit the family website; study other, similar websites to see how it can be better.	Teach piano to the grandchildren, if they are interested.
Perhaps write a memoir, to be posted on the family website.	Redo the landscaping and keep up the outside of the house myself, in part for exercise.
Upgrade my computer when I retire, adding the newest graphics software and hardware.	Upgrade the inside of the house; make it warmer, cozier; paint the upstairs, new toilets.
Take classes in advanced graphics software, and possibly hire a tutor/mentor as I progress.	Take over the choir directorship from Madge when she retires.
Explore possible business strategy consulting—self-employment on selected days and months each year, working a maximum of 60 days annually.	Learn ballet and tap. Classes or a teacher. Maybe try out for older dance parts in musicals.

The Details

Rick and Mary Jean each took a week to finish their dream lists, select the top items, and put them in a rough time order. Neither had spoken with the other about the contents so both were eager to see what the other had listed after they finished a long walk in the park and sat at an isolated picnic bench to do the second phase.

They exchanged top commitment lists. Both smiled at where they had overlapped. Some of the other items raised eyebrows.

They put checks by similar dreams on the two lists, and Rick began filling in the top part of the form. Most of the seven shared dreams had to be rewritten.

The first brought a typical, "Of course, why didn't I think of that?" response from Mary Jean. "I just assumed we'd be married forever!" Still, they talked about it for several minutes, and both suggested the "seeking assistance" insert.

"The best way to make that happen is to schedule some 'us' time every day, Rick," she added, pointing to her own pledge to set some time aside daily to be with him. They agreed to make it 30 minutes, and figure out later which 30!

Both concurred that her mother's rapid decline had pushed that to the top of the action list. She was failing quicker than they had realized and needed much more personal attention. They worked on the wording of who would do what, and said they would begin by talking with Mrs. Alston on Monday night, then get the rest in place next week so she would move in within two weeks. Both were relieved to finally be in agreement on what to do and when.

They had talked about a weekly date several times so that idea was warmly embraced.

Both wanted more consistent vacations, while they could still hike and explore. Mary Jean wanted a commitment to go abroad, which Rick had done often before they married. Now he preferred camping nearby. So they tentatively agreed to go overseas one year, camp and hike the next, and so on until she had seen the five locales listed. Rick threw in New Zealand, and held out on Spain and Portugal until they had visited the others. Done.

Rick hadn't put contact with his parents high on his list but Mary Jean felt that time was running, his folks were already in their years, and the kids really didn't know them well at all. So he agreed that it was a good idea and should be done sooner rather than later. Mary Jean volunteered to engineer that reunion and follow-through.

Mary Jean said that since they attend most of the theater performances anyway, let's bite the bullet, get season tickets, and program around it.

And Rick was surprised at his wife's interest in the hospice program, since he too was impressed by it and felt he could help them organizationally. But he had forgotten it when he was groping for possible volunteer work. A warmly approved compromise, particularly since they would be using its services soon for Mary Jean's mother.

They were pleased with the others' personal dream lists too.

Mary Jean was especially surprised at Rick's top item, to visit more with their kids. Since she had lots of contact with both of the kids, she wasn't aware that Rick felt a separation, and was pleased that he would make this effort on his own.

Rick had no idea that his wife wanted to learn ballet or tap, much less that she wanted to dance in musicals! He thought she didn't like to dance at all.

He liked the other ideas, and was delighted that she wanted to handle the landscaping and interior decorating, both near the bottom of his preferences now and always!

Rick and Mary Jean had each come to the park with trepidation. What if the other really wanted out? Or had some harebrained and wildly embarrassing plan in mind?

How about us? What if we had found that our mate proposed some real conflicts or areas of true discomfort? Like one wanting to burn bridges while the other wants to build them? Or your mate wants their two batty sisters to move into your kids' just-vacated rooms?

In the next chapter, let's look at a rather simple process for quickly resolving conflicts. It's not magic but it is effective. It can also be applied when one reaches an action impasse when putting the dreams in motion...

Why bother to collaborate on a future life plan with your mate? Why the hassle?

Better to do this now than to find ourselves out to pasture, both running as fast as we can in different directions! Or worse, one running, the other just sitting.

It makes sense to get in sync because the future will come for us, alone or with mates, whether we plan for it or not. Most of us don't plan our first lives; we react. But we're older now, with learning and street smarts and living bruises. So why not consciously and collaboratively plan together for a Great Second Life that will make our kids and friends froth with envy?

Chapter 11

Conflict and Inertia Resolution

*There are two obvious kinds of conflicts. The first is between
protagonists, even mates. The second is between action and
inertia.*

*This chapter suggests a dandy tool that can resolve those con-
flicts quickly and satisfactorily.*

*One example of that first kind of conflict might involve
$500,000 worth of dreams next year and a $5,000 dispensable budget surplus to pay for them. Or a spouse who refuses to visit Rome and that is #1 on your must-do list. It
can be two top priority events on the same day in distant
locales. Without a tool to help resolve such impasses now
or when they occur, your second life plan can quickly grind
to a halt.*

*The second kind of conflict is more beguiling. You simply never
get started. Not that you don't want to: you've made a sin-
cere top-level commitment. You just haven't sufficiently
analyzed all of the necessary action steps required to fulfill
that commitment. Thus you haven't discovered the reasons
why you can't or won't comply, so you don't know how to
offset them with solutions that will make that completion
possible. Instead, you find yourself gripped by an inexpli-
cable resistance or a paralyzing inertia. It makes your
whole life plan seem like a cruel joke.*

*Two cures for the price of one! In this chapter you will learn a
straightforward technique to both resolve conflicts and dis-
arm resistance or inertia. Nor must you wait until your
later years to use it—it can be as easily applied to relation-*

ships or any other conflicts right now. It works at any time and for all ages!

Two potential hurdles scaled— and a lifetime technique learned!

In a perfect world...

In a perfect world we could do anything we wanted, without restraints. Our colleagues and our nation would cheer, God would smile, and the Nobel committee would call an extra session to create new categories to honor our many achievements.

But in the real world there's always some rub. Costs outrace dreams, *tempus fugit*, knees ache at three miles, and, damn it, we *are* going to die.

This chapter won't resolve the last, other than to help us fully fill the days (and nights) in between. Rather, it helps us take a hard look at the rub and gives us a powerful tool to at least smooth it out, if not cure it.

There are conflicts and there are conflicts. Some are obvious: shouts, fists flying, sputum spat, anger swallowed. And some aren't obvious: steps not taken, inaction driven by indecision, anger also swallowed.

How does that affect our second life plans?

The obvious conflicts first

These usually involve choices to be made. We have a tight June budget and three fun or noble opportunities that collectively require twice as much money as we have on hand. Or two events on the same day. Or we must program work, exercise, parenting, gardening, a brake drum replacement, a bit part in the

community theater play, and cheering on a neighbor at the yo-
deling semi-finals, most of it, it seems, simultaneously.

Solutions are equally as obvious. Flee to the cabin and an-
nounce glumly that "the pains" have returned. Or do things
chronologically until we drop. Or stomp around bellowing
about aliens or injustice ("If only...") until others ask us to quit.
Alas, most of us just nibble off what we want to chew, or must,
or can't avoid. Ultimately, unpalatable solutions, if solutions at
all.

Let me propose that conflicts be elevated to a different
plain. (This thinking isn't original. You will find it much more
fully developed by Drs. Robert Wubbolding and William
Glasser in their discussions about "Control Theory" and "Reality Theory." I'm merely applying the concept here to our second
life planning.)

It starts by asking "What do we really want?" We've begun
to do that for our second lives by creating a dream list, then selecting the key dreams and putting them in some time priority.
The solution also asks, beyond the dreams, what kind of person
do we want to be as the dream comes true? What kind of image
do we have of ourselves at that moment? Finally, it suggests
that we become proactive in our decisions to make that picture
materialize or to make our actions that support that image a
reality.

There are two worlds, the world we want and the present
world as we perceive it. They are rarely the same.

Using Rick's plan, he wants to maintain closer contact with
his children. He listed it because that's not happening now, it
probably never was as good as it might have been, and, if things
stay as they are, it will probably never get any better.

What kind of exercise will help resolve this dilemma?

He makes a three-columned list, labeling the columns
"What I want," "The Gap of Resolution," and "What I have."

CONFLICT RESOLUTION SHEET / Date:		
"What I want..."	"The Gap of Resolution"	"What I have..."

Then Rick fills in the first and third columns, leaving the middle column blank. Note that he digs deeper in defining what he wants. What he really wants is emotional closeness. And he wants a bond from the outset with his grandchildren. In his dream-making, he simply listed the things that he might initially do to make that begin to happen. (Rick might later rewrite that dream to bring it closer to what he really wants.)

CONFLICT RESOLUTION SHEET / Date:		
"What I want..."	"The Gap of Resolution"	"What I have..."
To get emotionally closer to my children, to bond better, and to know them as full adults. I also want to be a fully-involved grandfather from the outset.		Not much, really. I was absent both physically and emotionally when they were young so they sought their emotional support from their mother. Now I am acknowledged but largely ignored, except as the occasional disciplinarian.

The hidden barriers

The next step is to expand upon (or explain) the third column, as you perceive the difficulty at present. This is how Rick sees what he has now:

1. I was mostly building up the business as the kids grew up. I was usually at work or traveling. Sometimes I attended their sports activities but was probably too critical of their imperfections. I tried to get home for supper or at least well before they went to bed, but I was tired and at the least resistance from them (like a closed door) I didn't persist.
2. Before that, when they were born I was even busier, earning my spurs in my first job, then mostly on the road selling for five years in my second job. I tried to have some quality time with them when I was off the road but there was never enough of it and it was strained.
3. Neither of us saw much of them once they went to college, other than at the holidays. They seldom spent summers at home either, working at Yosemite and Glacier most of the time.
4. Both returned home for a while right before they got married, but they were busy with that and they were naturally preoccupied. I couldn't dent their defensive shells much, if at all.
5. Now they are married and busy so Mary Jean and I see them sporadically at best. She has gone to help as the grandkids are born but I can stay only a day or two.
6. I see now that if I don't step up quickly the same pattern will happen with my grandchildren. Since they are still infants, now is the time to share my love much more directly and openly with them.

As we look at Rick's desire and the reality, there is a true gap to be crossed. And the difference between Rick's perception of what he has now—column 3 above—and the first column, what he wants, is simply too great for him to close without some overt acts and some behavior modification.

What hides in that "Gap of Resolution"—column 2— are the behaviors and emotional responses (like anger, confusion, sense of abandonment, and frustration) that stopped Rick from creating and maintaining the close emotional contact that he wants now.

One way to start closing the gap is for Rick to spend years analyzing these behaviors and emotional responses *ad nauseam*.

Or Rick can simply ask, "What can I do now to make this dream happen? Rather than railing reactively and just giving vent to those emotions (and thus maintaining the status quo), what proactive steps can I take right now to bring us closer together and keep it that way?"

To cross the gap, this is what Rick decides he can do.

"I must switch to proactive, personal responses from my current reactive, external responses. Those simply keep things as they are.

"Of course, if either or both of my kids would contact me and ask that we draw closer together, or would live closer, or would stop being so busy and direct their attention my way, or would start sending notes and cards to me, or would take jobs with my company or in my field, or would spontaneously start coming home regularly, or if Melinda would make it a point of putting the grandkids near me whenever possible, none of this would be an issue. We'd grow closer. But I know that 'if only…' are fatal words. Like they are the problem and I'm an innocent victim!"

Rick is doing the right thing by putting as much down as he can in black and white. That's the first step on the path to resolution, or at least understanding—putting it in words so that any objective eye, and heart, can gaze upon it for cloud-clearing clarification. Then changing his attitude and behavior to create what he wants.

Rick must also accept the fact that just because he wants something very badly it may not come true. In this case, it is possible that he has so alienated his children that nothing he does will work, however positive and well meaning. But he doesn't accept that now.

He knows that some things won't change. They will likely always live some distance apart, they will always be busy, and it is too late to repair a childhood. But there are things he can do. According to Rick:

1. I can call Melinda and Rick Junior and apologize for having been a distant, and probably in their minds a "rotten," father.
2. In Melinda's case, I can tell her that I really am sorry that I was such a distant father, that she must know it wasn't because I didn't love her. It's too late to make excuses now. But it's the right time for me to be a great grandfather to her kids, and through that to get to know her better too. That in part I'd like to keep in much closer contact with her and her family now and in the future. I could ask how we could do that, if she's in agreement that it's a good idea.
3. If she rejects the idea, or shrieks and slams down the phone, I will have to either reconsider my wishes or pursue this question in other ways. If she is in agreement, I will implement her ideas, if they make sense and are doable.
4. Since Rick Junior and his wife are still childless, I can use the same approach as above but emphasize that I want to repair the distance between Rick and me now so that when or if grandkids come, I can be a super grandfather to them.
5. All of the above will be done after talking at length with Mary Jean, who knows how much I love the kids but is also painfully aware of the effects of my not having been present with them during their youth. I will discuss my actions with her, and ask for her support, asking only that she allow me to contact our kids first and take the necessary proactive steps before she provides whatever support she feels is appropriate.

6. Since both of my kids are active computer users, I will increase my e-mail contact with them.
7. I'd like to either visit them or have them visit Mary Jean and me at least once a year, and I'll help them with the travel costs, if needed, when they come our way. I'll also free up my schedule during their visit to be with them and my grandchildren as much as makes sense.
8. I'd also like some one-on-one time with both Melinda and Rick Junior, perhaps at a lunch or supper (or where we mutually decide) every four to six months, simply to get to know them better. I'll gladly travel to where they are or, if they are nearby on their own trip, to that place.

Rick might make this list half as long again after talking with his children. Or it may be shorter. Or nothing may be doable at all. The most important thing is that he is taking action. That he has clarified what he wants, what the current reality is, and he has at least an initial path to follow.

Rick's sharing with Mary Jean is critical, for her help in clarifying the past and present and for her continual support in the future, when needed.

Then his direct contact with each child is vital, to establish a clear line of communication and the working out of actual steps that he (and they) might take.

The rest is the persistent doing.

What about overlapping dreams?

What if you and your mate had a future conflict that involved overlapping dreams, would the same process or exercise help?

Let's create a low-octane conflict out of whole cloth to see how it might work.

Let's say your mate wanted to travel to Toledo to see her folks, she wants you to come with her, you were planning to run your age in kilometers (let's say 55, which is about 33 miles), you were counting on her logistical support—and both overlapped on June 23. That is the date of her family's annual reunion and, by chance and for a whole series of odd reasons, the only possible date you can make the run that summer. Neither are life-saving acts but both are important to each of you.

In a perfect world, you would each fully support the other, you by at least applauding her attending the shindig (if not participating with her), she by helping man the drops during your run and shouting madly as you broke the imaginary string. But in the real world, you will be many hundreds of miles apart that day.

Of course, one or the other could reschedule. But in our scenario that isn't possible. Instead, rather than creating some emotional impasse or anger, if each of you will list every problem that might occur that could prevent you from doing what you had planned, you can then work together to proactively solve them.

In this case, her going is no conflict at all. You both want her to go, you are sorry that you won't make it this time, she understands, and there are no other obstacles, like finances or health. All that's left for her is the going.

On the other hand, you are still left with a problem that could imperil your realizing your dream. That is, the lack of logistical support. Thus:

CONFLICT RESOLUTION SHEET / Date:		
"What I want..."	"The Gap of Resolution"	"What I have..."
To run 55 kilometers on June 23.		No logistical support during the run.

If you will acknowledge that mostly you want her to witness and applaud your singular feat—there is little more heart warming than watching your aging mate for hours on some back-woods road gasping for air and stepping on his tongue—and you can assure her that you refuse to drop dead at about 54.8 kilometers, your perception of difficulties in that third column from your achieving "what you want..." suddenly looks more manageable. These would be the conditions you'd have to re-solve to run the 55 kilometers:

1. You will need some defizzed Pepsi and water about every five miles, plus a banana at the second and an oatmeal cookie at the fourth location.
2. You'd like a shirt and headband change at about 16 miles.
3. If your running flats cause blisters, you'd like a second set of shoes available when needed.
4. You'd like to have somebody witness the start, finish, and that you completed the distance actually running.
5. You may need a sag wagon to bring you home if you can't make the distance.

Alas, that list looks far less imposing on paper than if left undefined in the mind. In fact, it's embarrassingly clear that with a bit of ingenuity you can do all five without your mate. All that's missing are the details. A revised column 3, with those details, might look like:

1. You'll run a 16.5-mile route twice, returning each time to your house. Thus you will need hidden caches at about 5, 10, 20, and 25 miles—except that 5 and 20 and 10 and 25 will be the same cache. All you must do is hide the plastic bottles and banana or cookie inside a small box behind a tree or bush near the road, with a small red marker on the street to tell you where the cache is hidden.
2. You can change clothes or even shower, if you wish, at the half-way spot at your house.
3. You'll know by the time you get home after the first loop if you need to bandage your feet or change shoes.

4. Maybe you will tell a neighbor to witness the run's completion, if it's still that important. At least you will know you ran it!
5. A friend of yours will be home that day and you can ask him if he'll pick you up if you call. There are at least five public phones along the route, so you'll carry 50 cents in a pocket. Anyway, you won't be down long. The residents will spot the vultures and will surely notify the police.

Incidentally, since it's this simple to logistically organize, why not run in Toledo? Or if you want to die of boredom there or at home, why not divide 55 kilometers by ten or five, and measure out a loop that size, passing your house at the end of each loop until you finish, again at home, at 55? No caches and everything you need will be at your house about every three or six miles.

You'd have the same result once you put in the foot labor.

The point: breaking potential conflicts down into their vital components using the three-column process usually leads to a mutually supportable resolution.

How does this help before-the-fact?

Usually there's a reason why folks don't just jump into realizing a dream, particularly when they've gone through all of the steps we have to put them down and spell them out. It's that they haven't thought through the negatives sufficiently well to have cleared a path for action.

Let me use another example that was regularly suggested by participants in my Second Life workshops as a future dream or goal, and is also one of my dreams: "I'd like to see a minimum of two live plays or concerts each month."

That seems straightforward enough, something that anyone can start immediately and extend into their dotage. But when I ask the workshop participants if they do that now, almost all said no. "Why not?" yields the proof that makes my point.

They usually offer three reasons:

1. Their spouse or companion won't go with them.
2. They never know what is currently being performed.
3. It simply costs too much money.

In other words, they love the idea and want to do it for years to come but they had never really figured out why they aren't doing it now. Which prompts me to suggest that our system will work just as well for unrecognized conflicts, to clear the air to make our future dreams doable the moment we wish to begin: at 48, 60, 71, or tomorrow.

Let's use the sheet once more, then look at solutions to each of these dream impediments after it.

CONFLICT RESOLUTION SHEET / Date:		
"What I want..."	"The Gap of Resolution"	"What I have..."
To attend two live plays or concerts each month.		Not doing so because of (1) no companionship, (2) no knowledge, and/or (3) no money.

1. Lots of options here: you simply go alone, you find another companion besides a spouse or a mate for one or both presentations each month. You join a theater or music club. Or you do some sleuthing as to why the companion says no. Is it the kind of play or concert? Is it the location, the hour, some hidden fear? Or is it their way or paying you back for not watching them play Senior Soccer? (Would staying awake during an occasional soccer game win back a companion to the plays?)
2. Finding out what is being performed is as easy as checking the newspaper or the weekly throwaways, getting on the theater mailing list, calling the theaters once a month, seeing

if there's a local website listing, and/or having your friends keep you informed.

3. Ever heard of ushering? You get a saved seat, have ushering companions, and it's absolutely free, if you'll gussy up a bit. Again, join theater senior groups, get a senior discount, see if they sell "rush" tickets at lower prices, go to the reduced-rate previews.

The problem is seldom finding the answers. Common sense, a few friends, and asking people knowledgeable about the topic will usually bring solid solutions. The problem is that we don't know what we don't know, and in this case it's those unthought of, hidden obstacles that prevent us from stepping right out and living our dreams even before their time.

What we have shared is a simple tool that helps us brush away the unseen emotional cobwebs or creates an arena for discussion and problem solving—or both.

It's not a panacea but it works wonders by asking, quite simply, "What do we really want? What precisely is our dream?" and then by asking, "What is going on right now?"

The magic takes place when we list our perceptions, then find and take the proactive steps that can make our dreams come true.

"Have you ever thought how solemn a thing it is to live? If you are grateful for your life, set a value on it: find out how much it is worth, and if it falls below what you would have it, begin to increase its value. ... be full of hope and love, and resolve to make as much of life as you can."

Ida Scott Taylor

Chapter 12

Converting Your Dreams into Action Plans

Here is where the dreams gain form and grit. Where they are pounded into realizable shape so humans can work them into their everyday living. Here they get some flesh and bone—and legs.

At the dream level, "I want to leave a legacy, a lifelong imprint on young scientists (or wayward teens...)" works just fine. It's properly imposing, lofty in direction, worthy of sacrifice, suitably vague. It inspires even the dream-maker as it's said or read. It makes the spirit soar and promises wee threads of immortality.

Alas, dreams needn't be that exalted. "Organizing the family Easter reunion" or "an uninterrupted hour a day of meditation or reading" are no less valuable or dreamworthy.

But none of them really mean much without some additional hard thinking, planning, and commitment. Most need some action retooling. Which is what this chapter is about. It explains a process and the means to convert the highest goals into doable action plans.

Dreams are hopes; they live in the mind and spirit. Actions are things done with the hands and the mind. We need both, but it's the doing that brings us the kinds of results (and those wisps of immortality) that can make your second life truly great. The magic is in the doing.

Hands-on work here, developing people-sized, real world action plans

Dicing dreams into edible bites

What makes dreams so hard to embrace and live is that they are so distant, so misty, so grand. It's hard to scale the face of the mountain on the horizon but no great task to climb a series of small hills that start a few hundred yards away.

So here we reduce the imprecise dreams to very precise steps, so that we know their components and, by knowing them, know how we can make those dreams come true.

One example will show what we've all experienced, that of putting something off and off because it seemed like so much work and we didn't quite know how to begin.

Some years back I was offering workshops to professionals about how to create and program their own seminars, some publicly but most to be sponsored by colleges or other institutions. About the middle of the program some daring soul would usually ask, "How do I make audio cassettes to sell to the people who attend my seminar?" I particularly remember it because I wanted to do exactly the same thing, make an audio tape, of the very program I was giving, to sell to others who lived thousands of miles away. But I hadn't the foggiest notion how. So I responded, "I'm about to do the same thing. I'll leave a sign-up sheet on the back table. Write down your name and address and when I figure it out I'll let you know the precise steps to take—by audio cassette!"

By the time they had filled up the third sign-up sheet, the clock was ticking. I had to live up to my promise.

So what I did was make two lists for my own use: one included everything I knew (almost nothing) about the process plus everything I could deduce by looking at singles and cassette series. The second list included every question I needed answered to be able to decipher the process and make it doable by others as ignorant as myself.

I then trotted off to the library—those were pre-web times—and I dug into the reference sources for anything I could find about audiocassette preparation, production, and sale. There was shockingly little. Worse than little. After the unintelligible electronics articles were subtracted, there was nothing—except the names of duplicators and some product reviews of tape machines for home use. (Remember, audiocassettes were still fairly new at that time.)

The instructions for the tape recorders were minimally helpful. But the companies that did the duplication had the answers—and wanted you to know them so they would have something to duplicate! I made an appointment with three duplicators (since I would need duplication of my tapes as soon as I could figure what to say on them and how to package them). They gave me reams of how-to advice and costs, plus addresses and phone numbers about where to buy V-cards, Norelco plastic boxes, labels, and mailers.

I bought an inexpensive tape deck, figured out how to connect it to my amplifier, where to plug in the microphone, how to position its holder to reduce unwanted noise, and how to get my voice recorded. It took hours of toying to get a good master and hours more to order the right packaging components. Days later the mountain was scaled and my first audio was created: "Producing and Selling Your Own Audio Cassettes." A free copy went off to those on the lists.

Which is the long way to say, I had a dream but it was just that. It only became a reality (and a very profitable, long-term income font) when I broke it down into its doable parts, then reassembled them so they fit my peculiar needs.

That's what we must do now with our dreams. Define each dream by the steps we must take, now or later, to make it doable. And in the cases where we are already doing part of that dream, how we can do it better or in a way compatible with our later vision.

Write your ideas down

Of all the steps we take in this book, this may seem the least necessary. "I'll just do it when the time comes," you say. "If I can do it now, I can do it then—and anyway, in this fast-changing world it will probably be all different when I'm one or many decades older. Right now it seems like just so much busywork."

I hear you—and flat-out disagree, although you're probably right that you will have to adjust your actions later to match the changes that will take place in the meantime.

None of us really likes change. And we're very, very slow about doing new things—a tendency that almost always gets worse as we age. So if we don't break down the process barriers now, many or even most of our dreams will probably remain as far from our everyday lives as they are today.

This process is also much like the tool for conflict resolution we just read. The largest part of that tool, to reduce resistance and inertia, is micro-defining the dream, breaking it into under-standable and easily doable parts, just as we are about to do here.

There's a powerful second reason too. Why wait years to enjoy your best dreams? Why not get started now, at least learn-ing the rudiments or buying the utensils? Getting a head start is far easier if you understand the basics of the dream first.

I recall reading about a bored high school sophomore who was ordered by his mother to take his grandfather fishing. He moaned and moped but finally agreed, mostly because he needed an adult in the car so he could drive. The boy had never baited a worm—nor, amazingly, had the grandfather! But they figured it out, had a lot of fun, caught some fish, and set up a weekly date to fish out all of the local lakes and ponds. I remember the article because the boy boasted to all of his friends that he'd taught his grandfather how to fish—and that he wasn't going to lose 60 years of fun like his gramps had!

Why lose any time at all? Why not nibble on those dreams, starting tomorrow? If cycling in the Rubberneck Mountains is a #5 dream, get a cycle and start riding. Or start training in the hills. You may find yourself in the Rubbernecks years earlier than you originally planned. (What do you do later when you had planned to conquer the Rubbernecks? Move over, Lance. Cycle in the Andes or the Rockies, or write books for cyclists visiting the places you most enjoy.)

Create an Action Plan for Each Dream

How much step-by-step breakdown do the dreams require? It varies.

If you are already doing part of the dream, your action plan may be quick and short: how will what you are doing now differ between now and then?

But if the dream is to take up fishing and you aren't sure if they fly or grunt, then there may be a dozen things to list and look at in this phase. As a rule, the less familiar and the larger the dream, the more details it will require.

Let's look at an easy form below that we can use to create an Action Plan for each dream.

On the first line, I'd begin with the date when you first complete the form, then every time you update or modify it I would change it to that day's date. Do it in pencil if you are handwriting the form.

Write down the dream itself in the most precise terms possible. Should you later discover that you only want part of that dream, or more than you wrote, just rewrite it. None of us are seers when it comes to dreams a decade or two off, but we must start somewhere.

The dollar box tells you how much the dream might cost you to realize, or how much it might reap in income. (Income from dreams? Are you going to write a book? Consult? Do handy-man projects in the neighborhood?) The "Financial Calculation" section further down offers a place to list the major financial considerations.

The core of this form is the "Action Steps" segment. This is where you list everything that must be done between now and when the dream is fully realized. It is the steps I wrote down, then followed to create my first audio cassette (though now it would be for a CD or DVD). Or everything you must do to be able to fully and enjoyably cycle the Rubbernecks.

This segment may be several pages long for complex, ambitious dreams, or only a few lines for something you are doing now but want to modify in the future. Put your best brainpower here. Then dip into these action steps whenever you want, to get a head start on your project.

"Health Considerations" is just that: what must be modified or at least considered in terms of its impact on your health. If you have type-B blood, think long before doing bloodletting things in the remote Indian areas of South America. It can't be found. (But if you're going to do it anyway, write that concern down.) If you're a tick or two from the mortuary, ultramarathons must be rethought, or provisions or concerns should at least be included in this box.

"Notes" are for anything important to the realization of that dream that should be shared, but doesn't fit in elsewhere. Or for doodling or creating time-prioritized checklists. Whatever else you need. That keeps all the thinking in one spot.

ACTION PLAN		Date:	
Dream:		**$**	
ACTION STEPS			
FINANCIAL CALCULATIONS		COSTS	POTENTIAL INCOME
		$	$
TOTALS		$	$
HEALTH CONSIDERATIONS			
NOTES			

If this is a library book, please do not fill in this page! For a free, full-page download of this form, see www.super-second-life.com/form12.htm

Examples with Action Steps

Let's look at items in Rick's Action Plans. We'll fill in the rest later.

ACTION PLAN	Date:

Dream: Become more proactive with Mary Jean's mother. Coordinate her moving in with us. Oversee her finances. Explore the hospice program for when it's needed.	$

ACTION STEPS

1. MJ and I have already created a tentative schedule for her mother (Mrs. Alston) to move in with us. We have moved the time up to begin within two weeks.
2. First, though, MJ and I must meet with Mrs. Alston on Monday to reconfirm her desire to live with us and to move within two weeks.
3. I will get containers for Mrs. Alston to pack her personals. I'll ask her to put "stickies" on those things she wants me to move to our house. The rest will go in storage.
4. The Jones boy will help me fill a rental truck with her belongings.
5. MJ will bring her mother to the house after she has identified which boxes go where.
6. Jones and I will give her apartment a final cleaning and return the keys to the landlady.
7. MJ will make her mother comfortable at our house and set up some ground rules: the back room and restroom are hers, we will install her telephone and I'll hook up the antenna to her TV, she will help with the cooking in the beginning (as long as she can and wants to), and her little dog can use the yard since we already have a doggy door into/out of the kitchen. The rest she can work out with MJ: shopping, going out, etc.
8. I will coordinate Mrs. Alston's accounts and bring together all of her financial papers, including insurance, Medicare, retirement pension, Social Security income, and dividends. I'll discontinue her utilities and pay the final apartment bills. She will continue to pay her future bills and use her checkbook, but I will need to see the stubs and the receipts every two weeks. Once a month she and I will go over her current financial standing.
9. Because Mrs. Alston has said that she will not live with us without paying part of the rent and food, MJ and I will work out a modest percentage and get her approval, so I can handle the funds in her financial accounts.
10. I will complete and mail Mrs. Alston's tax papers for this and, perhaps, her coming years.

11. Eventually, as Mrs. Alston has requested, I will pay all of her bills and handle all financial matters for her. She has already signed a limited power of attorney; later she will sign a full power of attorney. Her will is in order and she has signed a living will.

12. Since the doctor has said her condition is terminal, Mrs. Alston has asked to be able to spend her very last days in a hospice program, at our home or the hospital hospice setting.

13. After she has settled in for a few weeks, I will request Mrs. Kolinski to come to our home to speak with the three of us about how that program would work: when it would begin, where, the financial considerations, etc.

14. I will handle all coordination with the hospice group, including the bringing in of a special bed, etc.

15. Ultimately, Mrs. Alston has asked that specific organs be donated and the remains of her body be given to the local university for use by the medical school. That paperwork is completed. Upon her demise, I will call them and help arrange the transport. She wishes a small ceremony at her church, without the body present. MJ will contact the minister and will help arrange that.

Rick bumped this dream up to top standing because Mary Jean's mother's condition was diagnosed as terminal, she is beginning to enter her final stages, and she probably has less than six months to live.

While this is hardly in the "fun things to do in the future" category, Rick's dream is that Mrs. Alston have as comfortable, peaceful, and supportive a final living period as possible. Nor does he even have time to "retire" before it takes place!

All that said, it is a huge relief to Rick and Mary Jean that they were able to discuss it objectively and at length and are now able to calmly plan what each of them can do to make this passage smooth and as joyful as possible for all concerned. So that is what his action steps describe, in chronological order.

Here is a much happier dream.

ACTION PLAN	Date:

Dream: Have a scheduled weekly date with Mary Jean. $

ACTION STEPS

1. This is more important now than ever before because I will be working long, hard hours these last three years to get the company's selling price as high as possible, and I've also been negligent in this regard recently.
2. This will also give us personal time alone now that Mrs. Alston will be living in our home.
3. In fact, Mary Jean and I talked about this for an hour the other evening, and both of us want to begin immediately.
4. We must define what constitutes a "date." Details must be finalized, but for now it means outside the house, alone or with pre-selected friends who are invited beforehand to join us—but not just fulfilling a social obligation, like attending a wedding or going to a company gathering.
5. Who will pick out the activity? We decided that since I am awful (read unimaginative) in this regard, Mary Jean will plan the first three dates a month and I will do the fourth (and if done on a certain day and there are five in that month, the fifth).
6. Since neither of us likes surprises much, we agreed that "mystery" sites or "surprise" dates will be kept to a minimum.
7. At the outset we have decided to budget $160 a month for this, in part to keep the activities from mushrooming into high-ticket items. I will pay and it will be itemized to our date budget.
8. If we substitute a fun weekend for a date, the first $40 goes to that special budget. We can agree that this will replace two dates; if so, the first $80.
9. Within the next few weeks, we will dedicate an hour to creating a list of the kinds of things we'd enjoy doing together. I will post the final printed copy on the kitchen board. I will cross off the things we do; we can both add any new ideas as they occur to us.
10. When the company is sold, we'll look back at these date activities to see if we found things we would like to expand into our future lives, as new dreams.
11. As we go along we will discuss how this is going and how it can be improved. We might also pick topics that we will agree not to discuss on the dates.

12. Unless agreed upon by the 8 a.m. the morning of the date, anybody who finks out must pay the other $50, no questions asked. From their own pocket, not the date budget!
13. We must work out the day (evening) of the dates or the specific dates each month. Ideally, a list of the activities we chose for that month will be known before the month begins. The date list will be kept on the kitchen board. Its maintenance is my job.

Another idea so good that it must be done now!

Actually, Rick and especially Mary Jean (who likes to dance!) have been dodging the issue of too little one-on-one time since the kids have left, so since the ice was broken as they exchanged their dream lists, this has been the hot topic of discussion. Why wait? They both agreed, particularly now with Rick pushing hard at work.

So what we read here are Rick's first thoughts about how this dream can get going immediately.

The biggest issue? "What's a date?" So they have precisely that, a date 15 days away, when they will go out for supper and talk about just that, plus work out the details for the first trial year. In the meantime, Mary Jean is dragging Rick to a barn dance. Date #1.

A third dream.

ACTION PLAN	Date:
Dream: Explore possible business strategy consulting—self-employment on selected days and months, working a maximum of 60 days annually	$

ACTION STEPS
1. This can't be done until the business is sold.
2. Ed Linden agreed, orally, that there will be no "non-compete" clauses in the sale of the company, knowing that I want to consult later. But he has asked that I not consult with the key firms that our present company competes with nor will I divulge non-public facts about our company, to which I readily agreed.

3. Ed also suggested an on-going consulting contract with me. I said that I was interested but it would be best to negotiate that after the firm is sold.

4. Now I intend to study precisely how the consultants we use got our business, the ways they negotiated their pay, the forms they use, and how they best serve us.

5. I plan to read two articles a month about negotiating, particularly by after-career advocates.

6. I plan to attend one or two workshops a year about this topic.

7. Next year I will increase my activities in (4)-(6), and in my third (and last) year in the company I will initiate steps to set up my own consulting company, identify specific or niche areas where I have singular expertise, and create a company plan, some preliminary info sheet or fliers, and my unique selling pitch.

8. I will also create both computer and paper files about consulting.

9. I won't openly discuss this nor will I approach a potential client until the company's sale is complete.

This is not a shared dream, of course, nor one that Rick plans to pursue immediately. But notice that he will be looking at consultants with a much more inquisitive eye from here on, as well as reading about what they do. His most aggressive act is to attend workshops about consulting. Rick is aware that Ed may indeed be wary of his consulting with the competition, so they have discussed this first. Rick has also decided not to discuss his consulting at all until the company has been sold.

Get the idea? The more we break these down now into digestible bites, the more likely they are to come true and the sooner we will enjoy them.

At the least, defining small, doable steps keeps us from foot shuffling and procrastination, then roiling in emotional and mental paralysis, then muddling in remorse after the fact because we did nothing.

On the more immediate and less dramatic side, it also helps us identify the financial impact each dream will create. And just in time, since that's the question we must answer in Chapter 13, "How can you afford all those dreams?"

Chapter 13

Can You Afford All Those Dreams?

That's the question you've been asking all along!

Dreams, schemes. Unless you can figure out how to eat, stay warm, dress at least decently, and pay for cable, what's this foolishness about also having a great life and super dreams?

Well, living our dreams is the reward we get for using our head, being a bit frugal all along, and for making plans about what we really want to have come true.

So here we add dollars and cents (sense) to the dreams to see what in fact we can afford, and when.

More important, if there are two of us rowing our lifeboat, how we can both realize our individual life dreams, plus those we want to share together?

This chapter won't grow greenbacks but it can help us see, even decades before, what kind of discipline and direction we might need to live the kind of full life we want and deserve after the heavy lifting is over.

It's time to guesstimate our way to a Great Second Life!

In Chapter 7 we devised a worksheet to see when we might have dispensable money available at various times during our second life. Now is the time to match those guesstimates with the things we'd like to have or do in our future. Here, we match our plans with our ability to afford them.

You ask, "Isn't this a bit like balancing 'maybe' dreams with 'perchance' cash? How can that be done with any kind of precision 15 or 30 years away, with 150 variables in between?"

It is imprecise, of course, but the action steps required and the approximate costs of each at least provide a general framework from which a future direction can be plotted and the necessary financial decisions can be made to help the best of that future happen. Without planning, we have no guidelines; with it, some coordinated, orderly energy can be directed toward laying the financial base for the kind of future we want.

Does that lock you in decades too early? Hardly. Your plans and the finances to afford them can be redirected any day of your life—but you must first know what they are to wisely change them. So let's start now...

Alas, nothing's free

No MENSA magic needed here. By the age of 40 or 50 we've fully grasped one of life's hardest lessons, that nothing is free, including lunch. The future is no exception, though it's now a bit freer with senior discounts for, it seems, nearly everything but senior services.

So we must find out if we will be able to afford our geriatric vices or if we will be limited to the thinnest pastures on some stony tundra for lack of spendable moolah.

Future money will probably come from three sources: (1) money we or our employers have saved for us during our youth or earning years, plus interest and/or dividends, (2) money we earned—or will earn during our "extra" years, or (3) surprise money, like an inheritance or our kids paying us back their childhood allowances (with interest), probably in the same miserly weekly increments we paid them. (Just so that repayment doesn't come with the same spending directives: "Don't buy anything stupid with this!" or "Be sure to put half of this in your college fund!")

As mentioned, in Chapter 7 we discussed building the necessary financial base to give us choices and some pecuniary freedom in our dotage.

In this chapter we again take a look at our Second Life Money Worksheets to see the approximate amount we will have available to spend.

At the same time we must make a rough calculation of how much it will cost us (or the dream will bring us) to realize those hopes. We will include that calculation in the Action Plan "$" box.

When our wants exceed our means...

How depressing will it be when we find ourselves consigned to 30 years of utter deprivation because of earlier excesses or profligacy? Isn't it better not to know our future financial state until the heavy truth makes itself known?

Hardly! Debt prisons are out of vogue in America, there is a solid net to prevent starvation in the streets (or anywhere), and all you really have to do is dream differently, like swapping the latter-life Porsche of your dreams for a bus pass! Or a trip to Boise instead of Bangkok.

So this is the time to make the rough future calculations. If our needs are less than our ability to pay with discretionary funds, great. If we want more than we can afford, we have several choices:

1. We can want less—reducing the number of dreams or allocating less to each.
2. We can postpone them to a later time. But there can be a problem if we do that for too long!
3. We can earn some or all of the shortfall difference, probably by part-time working.

4. We can find a way to reduce the costs of realizing one or many of the wants, to afford more with less.

There's another thing too. This chapter has so far assumed we are entering our second lives alone. Yet most face "gift" years mated, so let's also address that later in this section.

The best way to evaluate our future financial status is to blend the Action Plans we are developing now with the financial worksheet(s) we created earlier.

Our Action Plans Full Fleshed!

We have just seen the following three examples. Now let's convert the Action Steps into costs or potential income. How do we do that? By listing any item that will cost or make money, with a guess at the amount. (For now, let's omit the earlier Action Steps but fill in the remaining four empty boxes.)

ACTION PLAN		Date:	
Dream: Become more proactive with Mary Jean's mother. Coordinate her moving in with us. Oversee her finances. Explore the hospice program for when it's needed.		**$ 105**	
FINANCIAL CALCULATIONS		COSTS	INCOME
Moving containers: will get free at supermarket		$	$
Moving: will use a neighbor's pickup truck		15 (for gas)	
Storage of excess items: Mrs. Alston will pay			
Jones boy: one day moving and cleaning		75 (+ $15 for pizza)	
Phone and TV connections: Mrs. Alston will pay			
Room and food: Mrs. Alston will pay			
Contribution to hospice: in Mrs. Alston's will			
	TOTALS	$ 105	$

HEALTH CONSIDERATIONS

Our health is not affected by this move. In fact, it is an ideal time since we are both hardy and eager to help her.

NOTES

The only concern is whether I will have the extra time to devote to her finances and taxes for the coming three years, until the firm is sold. But if I don't, I will hire an accountant who will be paid, ultimately, through Mrs. Alston's will. We will pay those bills, if they arise, in the meantime.

This is a poor example to show financial concerns because, other than moving Rick's mother-in-law (which may cost $105 by using a friend's truck, who owes Rick 100 favors), the rest of the out-of-pocket expanses will be paid by Mrs. Alston herself, at her absolute insistence. Her life expectancy is short, she has considerable savings and Social Security income, she is well covered by insurance, and Mrs. Alston has always insisted on paying her own way.

The other expenses, like driving her to the doctor or getting tax assistance to handle her estate, would gladly be paid by the Bensons anyway as part of their everyday budgeted costs.

ACTION PLAN	Date:	
Dream: Have a scheduled weekly date with Mary Jean.	**$ 1,920**	
FINANCIAL CALCULATIONS	COSTS	INCOME
We have decided to keep this to $160/month.	$ 160/mth	$
TOTALS	$ 1,920/yr	$

HEALTH CONSIDERATIONS

The only stipulations concern eating out, where I cannot eat chocolate or drink carbonated beverages and Mary Jean cannot eat highly-spiced food of any origin!

NOTES

We will see if our budget holds or if the monthly amount should be increased.

A bit under $2,000 a year for a date a week is a great deal! Since the Bensons are frugal anyway, hardly drink at all anymore, and are more impressed by good food than the ambience (though they'll gladly take both if that occurs), this number seems realistic.

They also plan to get two or three couples whom they enjoy involved on their dates, Dutch treat. That will add additional spark to the settings.

The third example is an apples and oranges list: some of the costs are for the coming year, some for the third year) and the income won't begin for at least three years. So Rick must budget and pay the costs as they occur and reimburse the family kitty later.

ACTION PLAN	Date:	
Dream: Explore possible business strategy consulting— self-employment on selected days and months, working a maximum of 60 days annually	$	
FINANCIAL CALCULATIONS	COSTS	INCOME
Lunch with friends who consult, for starting info: 5 x $50@	$ 250	$

1.5 workshops a year about consulting	400	
Hotel (3 x $100), food ($100), travel ($500)	900	
DBA cost when set up company (third year)	75	
Develop personal library about topic: books and tapes (first year)	700	
Goal: 60 days/yr, starting at $1,000/day		48,000
After sale, annual retainer with Ed's firm (equal to 12 days)		12,000
TOTALS (1st year)	$ 2,250	
TOTALS (3rd year)	$ 1,375	
TOTALS (4th year)	$ 1,300+	$ 60,000

HEALTH CONSIDERATIONS

None at present. If any develop, I will adjust the consulting days.

NOTES

Later, when consulting begins, I must create a Business Plan and determine projected annual costs versus expected income. Will I operate out of the house (perhaps Mrs. Alston's room)? Need a phone and fax/Web line? Part-time secretarial assistance? New attire? I can begin this after I talk with colleagues now consulting and hear/read the advice of experts.

Incidentally, $1,000/day is on the low side for an experienced consultant, even starting, so this is likely to increase rather quickly. The firm normally paid between $1,000-3,000 a day, with about $1,600 average. Must reconsider the starting rate when the actual date gets closer.

Rick must also determine, or develop, a unique area of consulting so he can gain some experience in it between now and the time he sells the firm, to add more credence and value when he later markets himself.

Why bother to list our costs when the plans are long from becoming reality? Because we must start budgeting somewhere with solid numbers or, being mortals, later we will have no idea where the odd totals came from or how they were derived. It's far easier to modify than to conjure up lost ciphers.

And listing potential income, isn't it as shaky? Sure. We may never earn a cent or we may decide that the whole topic is folly, but it is good to put our thinking and expectations on paper at the present. They usually provide the spark needed to get a new endeavor afoot.

A Time Line is Needed Next

An Action Plan floating in some future year tells you only one thing: the amount of expense or income you will have from that dream at that time. What you need to know is what you will be doing that year—which Action Plans will be in effect—and how much money you may have available to finance both your living expenses and your Second Life dreams.

You can do this for yourself (particularly if you will be living alone then) or, while you're at it, create a Time Line for you and your mate. Since we are using Rick and Jean's example here, let's do the latter.

The Time Line is nothing more than a guesstimate of when you and your mate prefer to live your individual and joint dreams.

We see that Rick has a Dream List ten dreams long, which he has numbered 1-10. Mary Jean has eleven, numbered 1-11. And together they have eight, which they have identified by the letters, A-H.

Further, between 2005 and 2010, Rick has two dreams he wants to explore, they have a joint dream, and Mary Jean, who wants to continue working during that time, has delayed her dreams until the next five-year period.

Time Lines can be drawn for each year, five-year periods, decades, or whatever period you wish. Here we are looking at a full 30-year Time Line, broken into periods of five years each. Because of space constraints, numbers and letters are used here and would be inserted into the respective Action Plans. But you may prefer to use a word or two for each on your own Time Lines, for quicker clarity.

Second Life Plan Time Line

Rick	Both	Mary Jean
2005		
1 2	A	
2010		
3	B	1 2 3
2015		
4 5 6	D E F	4
2020		
7	G	5 6 7
2025		
8 9	H	8
2030		
10		9 10 11

If this is a library book, please do not fill in this page! For a free, full-page download of this form, see www.super-second-life.com/form113.htm

Finally, it must be repeated, then repeated again: dreams are not frozen in time because they appear on the Time Line at a certain point. They can be moved forward and backward, added to, dumped, whatever. They are dreams.

What's missing so far is the sense of financial restraints. As we will quickly see, the Bensons will be able to afford to do what they want, within the bounds of modest frugality, after Rick's company sells. But most of us aren't that lucky.

Integrating Your Action Plans and Second Life Money Worksheets

Once we have an idea when we'd like a dream to begin, we can see if it's fiscally possible by creating a Second Life Money Worksheet, as explained in Chapter 7. That will tell us, if we have some cost for the dream, whether we might have the dispensable money to finance it.

What might that completed sheet look like for Rick and Mary Jean? Let's use an arbitrary year, say, four years hence, the year after Rick sells his company.

Second Life Money Worksheet **Date:** 1 year after sale of company		
Annual basic living expenses	A	$ 50,000
Annual basic income:		
Mary Jean's annual net teaching income	$ 47,000	
Annual Social Security income	$ 0	
Annual pension income	$ 0	
Other annual income: 10% of company sale @ yr for 6 years, with 7% interest	$ 57,066	
Other annual income: Investment income	$ 96,000	
Other annual income: IRAs	$ 0	
Total income (add totals above)	B	$ 200,066
Annual basic income deficit/surplus	A-B	+/- C $ 150,066
Monthly supplemental income needed	÷12	$ 0
Special second life expenses this year	(from Action Plan)	$ 4,515 D
Total money budgeted for this year	A+D	$ 54,515

Maximum income deficit/surplus	if C is -, C+D if C is +, C-D	E	+ $145,551
Monthly supplemental income needed	÷12	$	0
Additional income source(s):	Amount		
Income source: Consulting	$		$ 60,000
Income source:	$		
Additional income available this year	$		F
Total income deficit/surplus for this year	C + F		$ 205,551

A quick explanation of three of the items above: Mary Jean at this chosen year is still teaching, so her retirement fund is still untouched. Neither are receiving Social Security income yet. Nor are they old enough to cash in the $50,000+ they will have in IRA funds, without penalty—yet. Assuming Rick increased the net worth of the company 60% before it was sold (to $3.2 million), and he received a sixth of 10% of the sale plus 7% interest annually, that accounts for his $57,066. And if he banks $960,000 after taxes from 40% of the firm's sale, and receives a 10% interest rate on that, the $96,000 is accounted for. (His total equity, which includes the $960,000, his home, and other items, does not appear on this sheet until it is brought in as income.) Total money budgeted for second life expenses refer to moving Mary Jean's mother in with them (years ago), the weekly date, and potential expenses in setting up his consulting. If that is earning at maximum, the surplus will be greater than $205,551. If Rick is not earning from consulting, it is still a healthy $145,551.

We should all have numbers like that! And remember that these amounts are very approximate. The Bensons are set for life. They can pretty much dream without financial consequences.

We can simply add up the ballpark numbers for income and estimated expenses and have a rough guide for how we will do individually or as a couple at almost any year this way. Of course, the farther out we go the less precise the numbers are. If the margin is as comfortable as the Bensons', bingo. If it isn't, then we need to fill in all of the details in the Second Life Money Worksheet and look more closely to see if we have sufficient, or extra, money for the year. If not, that's when we start drawing on the equity—or figuring out how we can boost our earnings for that year.

The value of this form is that it allows us to get a mental grip on what we can do financially, and how we can trim sails or expand our views to fit a truly great Second Life into our probably limited budget.

Dream Budget Sheet

The one line that most directly affects dreams is "Special Second Life expenses this year (from Action Plan)." You need to know that amount to see how you might fare in that particular year.

That number for the year in question—in our example, it is $4,515—is simply the sum of the expenses that you, or you and your mate, want to spend that year on your dreams. Your annual basic living expenses appear in the first line of the Second Life Money Sheet.

You can create a simple tally sheet that will account for this amount, and as dreams are added, trimmed, expanded, or dropped, you simply adjust the tally sheet and the "Special Second Life expenses" line for the year in question. These can be plotted out for one year, five, 20, or any number you wish.

How might Rick's Dream Budget Sheet look for the year after he sells his company, when the three dreams described in this chapter were projected?

DREAM BUDGET SHEET			
Rick Benson / One year after selling the company / Date: 2007			
Dreams:	2007	2008	2009
Funds available after co-funded expenses are deducted	$ 4,515		
Expenses related to Mrs. Alston, two years deceased	$340		
Date a week with Mary Jean (amount increased to $240/mth and divided evenly on budget sheets)	$2,880		
Consulting expenses / income in "Additional income source"	$1,295		

Later, when Mary Jean "retires" and pursues her own dreams, this list will be the sum of both of their dream costs or dream-created income.

Getting in Sync Financially

As long as there is sufficient money to live as you wish and realize your dreams, knowing the amounts is sensible and enlightening but hardly a source of controversy. The rub comes when the dreams are greater than the purse.

If it's just you, you can trim or earn and bring the two into focus.

But when there are two of you involved and some dreams must be adjusted or deleted, who makes the sacrifice?

The answer to that surely differs with each couple and the importance of the dreams, but that is a great time to try the conflict resolution tool suggested in Chapter 11!

One thing is certain: working together from the outset to create a Great Second Life that both want and believe in contains most of the answers. That's because the common desire and the communication required to design the future life and dreams already establishes the means by which changes and resolutions can be reached. You're already talking to each other about important things!

Earlier in this book we suggested a retreat, or at least time set specifically aside, to create your Dream Lists. If a family allocation conflict arises later, that too is a special opportunity to set personal time aside, empower two good minds, and see how the "dream money" and the general funds can be made compatible.

Sometimes no dreams need be sacrificed at all. These questions might suggest other solutions:

1. Is it time to start collecting Social Security or a pension?
2. If so, can health insurance costs be reduced?
3. Do you have equity that can be converted into income?
4. Is it time to start spending your IRAs?
5. Can you lower your other basic living expenses?
6. Or is a part-time job possible, at least to cover the dream expenses?

Half the fun is defining the dreams. The other half is making them come true—and part of that is finding the funding. The absolute worst thing that can happen without money? No dreams. No worse than if you just grew old without any planning at all.

But if you're smart enough to plan, you'll figure something out. The tools described in this chapter should help.

Chapter 14

Your Final Plan—
What Do You Do Now?

*Here you are, the only person on your block who knows how to
create your own Action Plan to spiff up your extra 30 years.
But it's still just so many words and a rolling avalanche of
funny sounding forms, each a reason for abandoning the
whole thing and just quietly getting old without interference
or interruption!*

*Don't quit! You simply need an annotated checklist to help you
put the words into motion! Amuse and amaze your friends
by your cleverness and energy!*

*What is the first decisive action you take to spank life into your
newborn baby?*

*And how do you get used to referring to and carrying out an
Action Plan after 40 or 50 years of living by (or on) the seat
of your pants?*

*Old dog and new tricks. Alas, we all learn the tricks that we
want to learn. That's the clue.*

A checklist to put the
Action Plan together

A checklist

First of all, congratulations! You've read this far—a high sign
that you may, in fact, convert yourself into a bona fide enjoyer

of the full life, with action plans, priorities, and great expectations for a fun 30 extra years or more.

The thinking, deciding, prioritizing, planning, and putting all that down on paper doesn't just happen. It's done by winners!

Even if you baled out a couple of times—a huge bonus if you read this straight through!—you've (almost) reached the finish line. Now it's time to channel your excitement into a finished product.

What are the most important things that you must do to make this process work? Prepare a Dream List, then create Action Plans. Those are the heart, the legs, and the fun. Capturing fantasy, writing yourself in, then pulling it off.

So I'd slip off, without distractions or time restraints, and let my imagination wander. Don't worry if brilliance isn't instant. Start with what you're doing now that you'd like to continue doing, but better, forever. Add in the things you can't (or don't) do now but ring a happy bell. Include activities you see others doing that you admire and want to try. Forget the costs or even health concerns: those can usually be bent around a solid dream. And forget special skills or training that you think they have or you might need. Far more powerful is your desire.

When you run out of initial ideas or dreams, think in age boxes. We usually plan first for the 55-65 year period. Think too of the successive decades: what would you also like to be doing then? What do you see others in that age group doing that you'd like to try? And what can you do from 40-55 that will make the later dreams easier and more fun, as well as give more purpose and structure to those middle years?

What about all those other charts and boxes in this book? They make it easier to develop your Dream List and create your Action Plans. They are helpful stepping stones that lead you through the process of converting dreams and supercharging your last years.

Now we bring all the work together

So let's put each of those stepping stones into a check-off chart, with a quick explanation of how they fit into the Second Life process:

SECOND LIFE PROCESS CHECK-OFF CHART			
	Chapter / Item	Explanation	✓
2	"Me Now" List 1	The five lists help us see what we've	
2	"Me Now" List 2	done and learned, who we are now, and	
2	"Me Now" List 3	what we want to do later. A quick look	
2	"Me Now" List 4	at ourselves. They help pave the way to	
2	"Me Now" List 5	creating a more comprehensive and realistic Dream List.	
4	Second Life "In" List	What do we want to keep and/or build from in our later days?	
4	Second Life "Out" List	What do we want excluded from those later days?	
7	Second Life Income Worksheet	What we earn and gather now, and how we can change this when we wish in the future.	
7	Second Life Expense Worksheet	Where our money goes now, and may in the future. Shows where we can better economize when needed.	
7	Second Life Money Worksheet	The critical summary sheet. Can be updated at any point in the future. Needed for the Action Plan.	
7	Second Life Net Worth Worksheet	Shows what we are worth now and may be at key points in our future. Hard to plan not knowing this.	
8	Second Life Dream List	Without dreams, or direction, it's hard to plan a vital, fun, worthwhile future. The Action Plans start here.	
9	Commitment	We grade dreams by our commitment to live them, focusing only on the most wanted.	

9	Time Box	Matches dreams to rough age categories, so we can best use our ability, energy, and wherewithal to make our dreams happen at the most appropriate time.	
10	Our Future Life Plan	Helps get in sync with your mate, to determine if the dream is yours, theirs, or shared.	
11	Conflict Resolution Sheet	If needed, helps you resolve conflicts or get in gear and moving!	
12	Action Plan	One per dream, these are the core of creating our own Great Second Lives. They include the dream, cost, action steps, financial calculations, health considerations, and preparatory actions.	
13	Second Life Plan Time Line	Tells what we (and our mate) want to do when.	

Let others help

There might be another box to check: Are you sharing everything about your projected Great Second Life with others who care? Ask them questions, seek their advice, let them help you form your plans—remembering that, in the end, those dreams must still be authentically yours to create your own best life.

Why not do at least part of the project with a friend, or another couple, or even a group of friends from the same age bracket? Why row into the future alone? I'm constantly amazed at the synergy that takes place in my Second Life workshops: the energy that is created and the excellent ideas we wouldn't have known had we not been on the same quest.

The same with solutions to pesky, even strange, problems. The least likely person digs into their peculiar well of experience or the stories they've heard, and suddenly a novel answer to a knotty problem emerges.

The truth is, a bunch of us are going to grow old together, whether we want to or not. For part of our journey, why not tramp through the same forest with similarly aging *compadres*, if for no other reason than for the companionship? And why not map the path now, even though the trek for meaning, purpose, and fun is still a while off?

You can brag too. You're a winner!

You also have permission to brag about having laid out a plan with specific purposes for your own future. Just by doing that you have risen to the top of the ranks. You are proactively taking control of your life and doing precisely what you want to do, after decades of fulfilling your role as student, spouse, worker, parent, and community helper. You don't stop being the others, but in the second half of your life they become part of your larger design. They are choices you make, among many choices. They are vibrant threads in an exciting fabric that you—*you*—are measuring, dyeing, weaving, and wearing.

They are but part of a life where you have an understanding and control of your finances. Where you have finally assumed responsibility for your health, and built a life pattern that finds you using your body, mind, energy, and hopes as you wish to use them.

More than brag, post your dream sheets, in final Action Plan form, where at least you can see them daily, to remind you of that thread, that fabric, that is letting you live as fully and with as much direction and vigor as humanly possible. The alternative—just bouncing along, really out of control, reacting rather than planning, filling in your days with no real direction or purpose—is unthinkable.

Brag good and loud. You're planning and living a Great Second Life. You're a winner!

"Retirement is not the closing of an old door, but the opening of a new one. It is the exciting approach to an infinite variety of new testing of a man's ability, new stretchings of his mind, new releases for his energies and abilities. All that is required is that he must recognize new challenge when it presents itself, and accept it zestfully. If he has been doing this all of his life, it will be easier for him in the later years, but in one form or another the opportunity awaits everyone, if he will only seek it."

Clarence Randall

Chapter 15

Keeping Your Life Plan Vital and Fresh for 30 Years

We're almost done.

In today's world, nothing is permanent—except change. So we can expect that even the spiffiest turbojet Great Second Life Action Plan will need periodic review, modification, and updating. If for no other reason than the person writing the first version at 40 or 50 will only faintly resemble the person living it out at 70 or 90.

What looks reasonable yet challenging in the first draft might look stodgy and stale to a tripper of the light fantastic several decades hence. Or exhausting to a person whose new later-life loves are Toltecan novels and lawn bowling.

Fifteen years ago who could have imagined we'd be learning how to arrange 0's and 1's on a home computer so we could surf the Internet or create our own interactive websites? Who knows what newfangled things will delight us fifteen years from now, much less 30?

So this chapter suggests reviewing our Action Plans, sprucing them up, trimming them back, or pointing them in some new direction. It suggests specific times when that might be done, even rewards for our not only being the brightest person on the block but for being brighter yet by keeping current our Action Plans, and us.

If you're to be up-to-date, here's how to keep your Action Plans current

If we'll change in 30 years, so will our plans

Anybody wise enough to create his or her own second-life plan knows that it's an ongoing labor of love. Nothing built around a dynamic existence is ever quite done!

On these pages we have discussed planning for 30-plus years of a great future. Thirty years is the time, in reverse, that it took you to have kids and settle in a job, get married, finish your education, raise hell in high school (or wish you had), play ball, steal your first kiss, get lost in the museum on a school trip, memorize all 50 (or 48) states, learn to ride a bike and swim, take your first school bus ride, play with your brothers and sisters, and be your parents' fat-cheeked, gurgling pride!

Look at the astounding number of changes that took place during that time!

It's no different in the second half of our lives than it was in the first, except that now we can control many of the changes and appropriately respond to most of the rest.

Thus our Action Plans carefully put together at 45 or 50 will still provide us with a path and a direction at 65 or 80, even though the background and the tools, means, and maybe even the determination may be dramatically different.

In our Action Plan dreaming we started with mental images of how we wanted to be at certain points in our life. Now we must ask, are we fulfilling those dreams, despite, or perhaps because of, the changes? And what must we review, and perhaps modify or update, to bring us and those visions into a brighter, truer focus?

If a second-life plan needs periodic adjustments, is it a waste of time to even lay it out now? No more than it is to map out a trip days, months, or even a year in advance. The trip is the point, not whether the road is subsequently renumbered, a motel along the way changes its name, or when we travel we change our plan en route.

It's also much easier, with the trip on the calendar and the excitement generated, to modify the details. If we're still eager to take the trip, then leaving a day or a week earlier, driving in a van rather than a coupe, and zigging past Uncle Elmo's along the way are simply wrinkles of an already exciting cloth.

The alternative? What usually happens when we have no plan is nothing. We just stay home. It's the same in travel or life.

One day a year...

The smartest thing is to set aside part of one day each year to review our entire second-life program. To get out our sheets or call up the file on our computer and give it a thorough, detailed going over.

Whether alone, with a companion, or with some close friends who care, it's worth an hour, or several, to see what we've accomplished, what is pending, and how we are faring on our lifetime venture. A reward should accompany that doing too: a special meal, some festive outing, or a second annual bath.

Why not use our birthday as the chosen date? Or some special anniversary? (I won't suggest April Fool's Day!) Some date that has significance and won't slip by unnoticed.

That's also a particularly good time to review our financial situation, gathering whatever data needed to create a current status sheet to compare with the others from previous years. Then if adjustments need be made, the week or ten days following might be dedicated to righting our ship.

No less important is our health, so that might also be the day to schedule our annual check-up—or whatever a knowledgeable, wise bill of health requires.

It's good to stop at set intervals to see precisely how we are faring compared to the same time the previous year. Let's admit it, we're all going to die. But are we getting there as slowly, gracefully, and joyfully as we can? As much as possible, are we in control of our own destiny, or at least of the stops along the way? Are we eking out of every moment what we want and need, without preventing or impeding others from doing the same?

Dream update!

Review time is also a chance to reread our Dream Lists. Are some of those lesser dreams that never hit the action level starting to look particularly appealing? Are you dabbling in something new that might be worth a new Action Plan and some dedicated implementation? Is it time to put some fire under a listed, top-priority dream that just sits there—or is this the day to dump it, as an idea whose time never really came?

Are we using our money wisely? Is it time to shift financial allocations? If you're planning to leave funds to your children or others, is it time to think about starting that now, within the tax-free annual gift limitations, so they can use it to plan their own second lives—or enrich their early years?

By now you understand the process. There's no magic to updating, nor any reason to go through the steps, other than to suggest that deletions and additions to Action Plans at any time are as natural and welcome as new names on a family roster and old addresses penned out and corrected in your address book.

What else might we consider?

If you're like me, you have been experiencing a rising horror as the number of forms in this book kept increasing. Not only does it suggest more time spent completing forms than living your second life, it conjures up the certainty that the minute you finish creating your dream world, the papers will vanish and it will all be for naught!

Well, the forms are cumulative and if we've been keeping up, we simply had to add or modify an item as the chapters progressed, then enter that in the Action Plans. And if we hide the results in our computer, it is all recoverable if, heavens, the paper gods or the vapors dematerialize our penned opus. (Copiers provide a similar back-up security.)

Where can we keep our Time Box, Action Plans, and Money Worksheets?

Where should be put the final project? In truth, let's *not* hide it in the computer, where too often "out of sight is indeed out of mind."

Let's make it as visible as we can. This is important stuff for us and our future!

Why not the easiest of physical storage formats? Buy one or several 2" brightly-colored three-ring binders and either use or print your forms, dreams, and plans on three-holed paper—or hole punch it at the library or Kinkos. Less than $10 total. And if we print and post huge letters—**MY GREAT SECOND LIFE PLAN**—on the outside of the binder(s), it will look sufficiently threatening and goofy to the unknowing that our plans will remain eternally untouched (by others).

The binder(s) will also have plenty of space for photos of our dreams being fulfilled, play programs, volunteer awards, and our Nobel notification. And they will be in sight at all time!

Of course, if we want to be daily inspired, we can reproduce our Action Plans in huge type and paste them wherever we regularly look. For more such inspiration, I defer to your genius.

Final Thoughts and a Paper Trail

Some final thoughts in defense of not only planning our second lives but keeping many of the details in written, accessible form.

The planning, and fulfillment, serves as a powerful model to others, particularly our children (and theirs). It shows us to be active, bright, forward-looking people who assume responsibility and control of our own lives. The kind of model that we would have respected and honored (and perhaps did) had we seen it carried through with such diligence and joy by our folks or others.

The records can also provide a paper trail of our lives that can be read and hopefully admired by kin and others a hundred or a thousand years hence. If kept on a computer, they will be readily usable in some convertible format forever. What would we pay today to have just such a record of our earlier ancestors?

That suggests additional sections we may wish to include in our binder, such as all the genealogical information we have (or can create or tap) about our family; a copy of our birth certificate and other official papers; photos of our family members and snapshots of our home(s) and prime possessions; perhaps our annual tax and health examination reports; all references in the press, awards, and commendations; pertinent letters we wrote or received; even a personal recollection page summarizing the highlights of each year. Again, your genius will suggest much more ...

Our lives are at stake here. Without asking, we've been given a gift of 30 extra years. It's up to us to figure out what we're going to do with that gift. Ignoring it seems, at least, ungrateful. With a plan, we can extract many more drops of delight and share many more touches of love.

So the pages you've just read have proposed that each of us figure out ways to make our dreams come true in those extra 30 years—and, by keeping our plan consistently renewed, add new dreams and continually refresh and expand the old ones.

Congratulations!

My wish is that every one of your second-life dreams comes true and that you "extra" 30 years are chuck full of fun, joy, and purpose.

"I don't believe in retirement. What would I do? It would be very boring."

Julia Childs

Appendix

Contents

200 MORE IDEAS
FOR A
GREAT SECOND LIFE

There are literally thousands of worthwhile, exciting things to do during our second lives. Here are 200 suggestions, to add to the 32 in Chapter 8. (If you wish to share your best ideas, please e-mail them to dreamlist@super-second-life.com *and we will post them there under "Dream List" for your enjoyment.)*

act as a liaison for a CARE "Adopt a School" Program
adopt a pet
assist at a homeless shelter
assist the choir director or pianist/organist at church
be a site facilitator for the Special Olympics
be the radio-TV liaison for non-profit groups
become a baseball umpire
become a clown
become a commissioned fingerprint specialist
become a court watcher
become a crossing guard
become a history docent of the town for the schools
become a legal assistant specialist
become a liaison between senior groups and local educational programs
become a lifeguard
become a local charity fund-raiser
become a mime
become a notary public
become a private investigator
become a swimming/diving instructor
become a visiting school "grandma" or "grandpa"

become an ombunsdperson for the library, city, or local services
become an oral historian for city archives
become an usher: theater, concerts, sports events
become proficient at wine tasting
become the city site photographer for historical preservation
can food and share it with others in need
catalog the local flora and/or fauna
chaperone kids or pre-teens to museums
chaperone kids or pre-teens to sports events
chaperone youth on church missionary programs
coach for youth leagues
compete in senior Olympics programs
convert your family photos to digital
create a family newsletter
create a guide to city or county festivals or activities
create a guide to city or county recreational facilities
create a local cycling map
create a map of city or county beauty routes (with mile markers)

create a map of city or county bridal paths (with mile markers)

create a map of city or county hiking paths (with mile markers)

create a map of city or county running paths (with mile markers)

create a paid proofreading service

create a website for your city or library

create a written family genealogy

create an historical guide to city or county buildings and sites

create an historical guide to past city or county festivals or activities

create and hold a treasure hunt for your family or local groups

create computer support for city and county boards or groups

create your own website

cycle your age (miles or kilometers)

deliver meals to shut-ins (Meals on Wheels-type programs)

develop a home medical transcription service

direct the church choir

do extra-hand work for your church, like painting and carpentering

drive a bus for a local transport company

drive the school bus

fix old bicycles to donate to youth programs

focus on and effectuate one specific act of city beautification

form a musical group: band, quartet, etc.

form a senior writer's group

gather crop surpluses for use at welfare feeding programs

gather used instruments for schools or youth groups

get and care for a horse

handle public relations for non-profit groups

help at day care during church services

help at local swim meets (records / timing)

help at local track meets (records / timing)

help at local youth league competitions (records/timing, etc.)

help at other local athletic events, like triathlons, marathons, runs

help candidates running for office

help design and plant a city flower bed

help prepare meals for welfare programs

help seniors install their computers

help supervise playground and school recess

help teach a foreign language at school

help the Braille Institute

help the poor or elderly file legal papers

help the poor or elderly prepare tax forms

help transfer written records to digital form

help your minister with home visitations

host a senior's radio/TV program

join a barbershop quartet

join a drumming group

learn a new trade

learn and master Aikido

learn and master belly dancing

learn and master calligraphy

learn and master handwriting analysis

learn and master line dancing

learn and master listening

learn and master meditation

learn and master papermaking
learn and master T'ai Chi
learn and master yoga
learn and practice sustainable
  gardening
learn and practice time management
learn bookkeeping and offer your
  skills to non-profit groups
learn estate planning
learn fresh water kayaking
learn landscape drawing
learn Latin dance, like Salsa and
  Merengue
learn or play a musical instrument
learn photography
learn self-defense
learn self-hypnosis / autosuggestion
learn to build instruments
learn to build your own stock
  portfolio
learn to converse with your spouse
learn to knit
learn to paint
learn to play the guitar
learn to produce booklets to share
  your family writings with
  kin/local library
learn to put folk songs to a musical
  score
learn to repair household appliances
learn to repair instruments
learn to sculpt
learn to sell your writing to
  magazines and newspapers
learn to serve as a group facilitator
learn to throw and glaze pottery
learn to weave
learn to write grant proposals
learn vegetarian soapmaking
maintain an updated list of local
  child care programs
maintain an updated list of local
  youth programs

manage small rental properties
offer free proofreading for student
  writers
officiate at local youth leagues
organize a church singles program
organize a master family photo
  album
organize an investment club
organize church senior drama and
  music programs
organize the records or archives for
  a local group
participate in city site preservation
  programs
perfect your ballroom dancing
provide holding care for infants at a
  hospital or orphanage
provide library pick-up/delivery
  service for folks in hospital or care
  homes
quit smoking
read aloud to children at the school
  or library
research/write travel articles
  for/about the aged, challenged,
  women alone
run for city, township, county, state,
  or national office
sell your photos to magazines and
  newspapers
sew a family quilt
stack books in the library
take the elderly, children, or
  newcomers to the library
teach basic computer skills to
  seniors
teach children how to churn butter
  and ice cream
teach children to bake
teach children to knit
teach children to weave
teach devotional studies classes
teach do-it-yourself car repair

teach do-it-yourself home repair
teach do-it-yourself landscaping
teach English in an ESL program
teach inheritance management
teach job application skills
teach kids how to repair bicycles
teach or help at vacation Bible
    school
teach others how to can (or preserve)
    food
teach others how to create their
    website
teach photography to kids or seniors
teach reading in a literacy program
teach self-defense to seniors
teach Sunday School
train others to record local records or
    sites for the city or library
visit retirement or convalescent
    homes
volunteer for medical
    tests/questionnaires
volunteer for the Special Olympics
volunteer to help at a men's center
volunteer to help at a women's
    center
volunteer to help on school field
    trips
walk students to/from school
walk your age (miles or kilometers)
work as a dental or medical office
    receptionist
work at the polls
work on city, county, or regional
    beautification
write a column for the local
    newspaper
write a family history
write a novel
write a senior's column for the
    newspaper
write a syndicated column
write a TV script

write and sell greeting cards
write book reviews for newspapers
    and magazines
write grant proposals for non-profit
    groups
write how-to articles
write lyrics
write movie reviews for newspapers
    and magazines
write music
write poetry
write the history book of your town
    or county
write the history of your family's
    cars/vehicles
write the history of your family's
    homes
write the history of your family's
    pets
write the history of your family's
    vacations
write travel articles
write/publish about local artists and
    writers
write/publish about local historical
    events and sites
write/publish about local prehistory

LOCAL RESOURCES

Almost every county or region in the U.S. has a guide to local non-profit agencies and resources. And most of these, it seems, exist to help folks 40+. Your reference librarian will lead you to your community resources directory.

For example, in my county there is the ***Santa Barbara County's Comprehensive Guide to Public and Private Non-Profit Human Resources***. Listed in the SENIORS category are care management, seniors centers, in-house care, legal, legislation, low income (free meals, cottages, housing corporations), employment, out-of-house care, programs, psychiatric help, recreation, transportation, adult education, lawn bowling, parks and recreation programs, dancing, volunteering, nutrition sites, and the YMCA.

But it doesn't stop there because in the hundreds of additional listings are A.A., Alzheimer's, arts and crafts, assisted living, blood pressure, senior board and care, care-giving, clinics, clubs and organizations, barbershop groups, cards, congregate meals, and computer teaching and assistance.

If you want to contact national groups, to commune with other souls with interests as bizarre as your own, check your library's current edition of the ***Encyclopedia of Associations***. It lists groups dedicated to almost anything. A few listings: Shoplifters Anonymous, Museum Volunteers, Hearing Dog Project, and the Cage Bird Judging Association.

Want to travel, meet others your age, and not spend a fortune? Then check ***Elderhostel*** at www.elderhostel.org or write to 75 Federal Street, Boston, MA 02110 and request a copy of their huge, thick quarterly catalog—it features US and Canadian programs for three of the quarters, international travel each fall. About 2,000 colleges or institutions take part. If you're 55+, for about $350-450 a week (fees, board, room, and classes) you can learn almost anything anywhere, like opera, jazz, the Kentucky Derby, photography, trekking, skiing, pottery, or the history of Black Hawk.

The best local resources? Start at your town library, then the City Hall, Chamber of Commerce, the local recreation program, and your church. Ask each to suggest additional resources. You'll be amazed, as I was, at the bounty that is within reach or immediately accessible by mail, phone, e-mail, or the Internet. (No computer? Use the library's.)

GENERAL RESOURCES

In the three resource categories that follow—general, health, and finances—I am including associations or organizations with services of interest to those 40+. Where available, the listing includes the name of the group, address, phone, and website address (first enter: http://www.)

Administration on Aging, Eldercare Locator, 330 Independence Avenue SW, Room 4656, Washington, DC 20201 / (202) 619-0724 / nih.gov

American Association of Homes and Services for the Aging, 901 E St. NW, Suite 500, Washington, DC 20004-2011 / (202) 783-2242 / aahsa.org

American Association of Retired Persons (AARP), 601 E St. NW, Washington, DC 20049 / (202) 434-2277 / aarp.org

American Geriatrics Society, 770 Lexington Ave., Suite 300, New York, NY 10021 / (212) 308-1414 / americangeriatrics.org

American Public Human Services Association, 810 First St. NE, Suite 500, Washington, DC / (202) 682-0100 / aphsa.org

American Red Cross, 1621 N. Kent St., 11th Floor, Arlington, VA 22209 / (703) 248-4222 / redcross.org

American Society on Aging, 833 Market St., Suite 511, San Francisco, CA 94103 / (415) 474-9600 / asaging.org

Disabled American Veterans, 3725 Alexandria Pike, Cold Spring, KY 41076 / (606) 441-7300 / dav.org

National Aging Resource Center on Elder Abuse, 1201 15th St. NW Suite 350, Washington, DC 20005-2842 / (202) 898-2586 / elderabusecenter.org

National Association for Hispanic Elderly, 234 E. Colorado
 Blvd., Suite 300, Pasadena, CA 91101 / aoa.gov/directory
National Association for Home Care, 228 7th St. SE,
 Washington, DC 20003 / (202) 547-7424 / nahe.org
National Association of Area Agencies on Aging, 927 15th St.
 NW, 6th Floor, Washington, DC 20005 (202) 296-8130 /
 n4a.org
National Caucus and Center on Black Aged, Inc., 11220 L St.
 NW, Suite 800, Washington, DC 20005 / (202) 637-8400 /
 ncba-aged.org
National Council on the Aging, Inc., 409 Third St. NW,
 Washington, DC 20024 / (202) 479-1200 / ncoa.org
National Council on Patient Information and Education, 666
 11th Street NW, Suite 810, Washington, DC 20001 /
 nap.edu
National Council on Senior Citizens, 8403 Colesville Rd., Suite
 1200, Silver Spring, MD 20910-3314 / (301) 578-8800 /
 ncscinc.org
National Hospice Organization, 1901 North Moore St., Suite
 901, Arlington, VA 22209-1714 / (703) 243-5900 / nho.org
National Institute of Aging Information Center, P.O. Box 8057,
 Gaithersburg, MD 20857 / (800) 222-2225 / nih.gov
United Seniors Health Cooperative, 409 Third St. SW, Second
 Floor, Washington, DC 20024 / (202) 479-6973 / ushc-
 online.org

*You can also directly download a link to all website references
in the appendix at www.super-second-life.com/links.htm.*

HEALTH RESOURCES

Alzheimer's Association, 919 North Michigan, Suite 1000, Chicago, IL 60611 / (800) 272-3900 / alz.org

American Academy of Dermatology, 930 N. Meacham Rd., Schaumberg, IL 60173-4965 / (847) 330-0230 / aad.org

American Academy of Facial Plastic and Reconstructive Surgery, 310 S. Henry St., Alexandria, VA 22314-3524 / (703) 299-9291 / aafprs.org

American Academy of Neurology, 1080 Montreal Ave., St. Paul, MN 55116-2325 / (651) 695-1940 / aan.com

American Academy of Ophthalmology, PO Box 7424, San Francisco, CA 94120-7424 / (415) 561-8500 / aao.org/news/eyenet

American Academy of Orthopedic Surgeons, 6300 North River Rd., Rosemont, IL 60018-4262 / (847) 823-7186 / aaos.org

American Academy of Otolaryngology—Head and Neck Surgery Inc., One Prince St., Alexandria, VA 22314-3357 / (703) 836-4444 / entnet.org

American Association of Cardiovascular and Pulmonary Rehabilitation, 7611 Elmwood Ave., Suite 201, Middleton, WI 53562 / (608) 831-6989 / aacvpr.org

American Cancer Society Inc., National Headquarters, 1599 Clifton Rd. NE, Atlanta, GA 30329 / (800) 227-2345 / cancer.org

American College of Obstetricians and Gynecologists, 409 12th St. SW, Washington, DC 20024-2188 / (202) 638-5577 / acog.org

American Dental Association, 211 E. Chicago Avenue, Chicago, IL 60611 / (312) 440-7494 / ada.org

American Diabetes Association, 1660 Duke St., Alexandria, VA 22314-3447 / (800) 342-2383 / diabetes.org

American Foundation for the Blind, 11 Penn Plaza, Suite 300, New York, NY 10001 / (800) AFB-LINE / afb.org

American Heart Association, 7272 Greenville Ave., Dallas, TX 75231-4596 / (800) 242-1793 / americanheart.org

American Liver Foundation, 75 Maiden Lane, Suite 603, New York, NY 10038 / (800) GO-LIVER / liverfoundation.org

American Lung Association, 1740 Broadway, 14th Floor, New York, NY 10019-4374 / (212) 315-8700 / lungusa.org

American Optometric Association, 243 North Lindbergh Blvd., St. Louis, MO 63141-7881 / (800) 365-2219 / aoanet.org

American Podiatric Medical Assoc., 9312 Old Georgetown Rd., Bethesda, MD 20814-1698 / (301) 571-9200 / apma.org

American Tinnitus Association, PO Box 5, Portland, OR 97207-0005 / (800) 634-8978 / ata.org

Arthritis Foundation, 1330 Peachtree St., Atlanta, GA 30309 / (800) 283-7800 / arthritis.org

Cancer Information Service, NIC/HIH, Bldg. 31 10A07, 31 Center Drive, MSC 2580, Bethesda, MD 20892-2580 / (800) 4-CANCER

Epilepsy Foundation, 4351 Garden City Dr., Landover, MD 20785 / (800) 332-1000 / efa.org

Glaucoma Research Foundation, 490 Post St., Suite 830, San Francisco, CA 94102 / (800) 826-6693 / glaucoma.org

Huntington's Disease Society of America, 158 West 29th. St., 7th Floor, New York, NY 10001-5300 / (800) 345-4372 / hdsa.org

International Hearing Society, 20361 Middlebelt Rd., Livonia, MI 48152 / (800) 521-5247 / ihsinfo.org

Lupus Foundation of America, 1300 Piccard Dr., Suite 200, Rockville, MD 20850 / (800) 558-0121 / lupus.org

National Alliance for the Mentally Ill, 200 N. Glebe Rd., Suite 1015, Arlington, VA 22203-3754 / (703) 524-7600 / nami.org

National Arthritis and Musculoskeletal and Skin Diseases Information Clearing House, 1 AMS Circle, Bethesda, MD 20892-2350 / (301) 495-4484 / nih.gov/niams

National Digestive Diseases Information Clearinghouse,
2 Information Way, Bethesda, MD 20892-3507 /
niddk.nih.gov/health/digest/nddic.htm
National Eye Institute, 2020 Vision Place, Bethesda, MD
20892-3655 / (301) 496-5248 / nei.nih.gov
National Headache Foundation, 428 W. St. James Place, 2nd
Floor, Chicago, IL 60614-2750 / (800) 843-2256 /
headaches.org
National Institute of Neurological Disorders and Stroke,
P.O. Box 5801, Bethesda, MD 20824 / nih.gov
National Institute on Deafness and Other Communication
Disorders, NIH, 31 Center Drive, MSC 2320, Bethesda, MD
20892-2320 / (301) 496-7243 / nidcd.nih.gov
National Kidney and Urologic Diseases Information
Clearinghouse, 3 Information Way, Bethesda, MD 20892-
3560 / (301) 654-4415 / niddk.nih.gov
National Kidney Foundation, 30 East 33d St., 11th Floor, New
York, NY 10016 / (800) 622-9010 / kidney.org
National Mental Health Association, Information Center,
1021 Prince St., Alexandria, VA 22314-2971 / nmha.org
National Osteoporosis Foundation, 1232 22nd St. NW,
Washington, DC 20037-1292 / (202) 223-2226 / nof.org
Self Help for Hard of Hearing People, 7910 Woodmont Ave.,
1200, Bethesda, MD 20814 / (301) 657-2249 / shhh.org
Skin Cancer Foundation, 245 5th. Avenue, Suite 1403, New
York, NY 10156 / (800) SKIN-490 / skincancer.org
The Simon Foundation for Continence, PO Box 815, Wilmette,
IL 60091 / (800) 23-SIMON / simonfoundation.org
United Ostomy Association, 19772 MacArthur Blvd #200,
Irvine, CA 92612-2405 / (800) 826-0826 / uoa.org
United Parkinson's Foundation, 360 W. Superior St., Chicago,
IL 60610 / (312) 664-2344

*You can also directly download a link to all website references
in the appendix at www.super-second-life.com/links.htm.*

FINANCIAL RESOURCES

American Association of Individual Investors, 625 N. Michigan
Avenue, Suite 1900, Chicago IL 60611-3110 / (312) 280-
0170 / aaii.com

Association of Jewish Aging Services, 316 Pennsylvania
Avenue SE, Suite 402, Washington, DC 20003-1175 / (202)
543-7500 / ajas.org

Association of Private Pension and Welfare Plans, 1212 New
York Avenue NW, Suite 1250, Washington, DC 20005-
3987 (202) 289-6700 / appwp.org

Financial Planning Association, 3801 E. Florida Avenue, Suite
708, Denver, CO 80210-2571 / (303) 759-4900 / fpanet.org

International Association for Financial Planners, 5775
Glenridge Dr. NE, #B-300, Atlanta, GA 30328-5364 / (800)
945-4237 / iafg.org

National Association of Health Plans, 1129 20th St. NW, Suite
600, Washington, DC 20036-3403 / (202) 778-3200 /
aahp.org

National Association of Personal Financial Advisors, 355 W.
Dundee Road, Suite 200, Buffalo Grove, IL 60089-3500 /
(847) 537-7722 / napfa.org

National Organization of Social Security Claimants
Representatives, 6 Prospect St., Midland Park, NJ 07432-
1634./ (201) 444-1415 / nosscr.org

*You can also directly download a link to all website references
in the appendix at www.super-second-life.com/links.htm.*

"ME NOW" LIST 1		
Contributions Achievements Activities	Skills Developed	Ways I might apply these skills in my second life...

If this is a library book, please do not fill in this page! For a free, full-page download of this form, see www.super-second-life.com/form2A.htm

"ME NOW" LIST 2		
An objective person would use these adjectives to describe me now	Adjectives no longer applicable that they might have used about me in my first life	New adjectives I would like them to properly use about me during my second life

If this is a library book, please do not fill in this page! For a free, full-page download of this form, see www.super-second-life.com/form2B.htm

"ME NOW" LIST 3	
These 10 words describe my first life:	I'm putting an "X" by those that I want to continue to describe my second life
1.	
2.	
3.	
4.	
5.	
6.	
7.	
8.	
9.	
10.	

If this is a library book, please do not fill in this page! For a free, full-page download of this form, see www.super-second-life.com/form2C.htm

"ME NOW" LIST 4		
These are attitudes, activities, traits, etc. that I want to leave at the gate	These are strengths I now possess that I want to take into my second life	These are strengths I want to develop in my second life

"ME NOW" LIST 5

These 10 words would add joy and worth
to my "Great Second Life"

1.	
2.	
3.	
4.	
5.	
6.	
7.	
8.	
9.	
10.	

If this is a library book, please do not fill in this page! For a free, full-page download of this form, see www.super-second-life.com/form2E.htm

SECOND LIFE "IN" LIST

What you want to include in your Great Second Life:

1.	
2.	
3.	
4.	
5.	
6.	
7.	
8.	
9.	
10.	
11.	
12.	
13.	
14.	
15.	
16.	
17.	
18.	
19.	
20.	

If this is a library book, please do not fill in this page! For a free, full-page download of this form, see www.super-second-life.com/form4A.htm

SECOND LIFE "OUT" LIST

What you want excluded from your Great Second Life:

1.
2.
3.
4.
5.
6.
7.
8.
9.
10.
11.
12.
13.
14.
15.
16.
17.
18.
19.
20.

If this is a library book, please do not fill in this page! For a free, full-page download of this form, see www.super-second-life.com/form4B.htm

Second Life Income Worksheet / Year or Age:

INCOME	(1)	(2)	(3)	(4)	(5)
(1) Annual / (2) Monthly / (3) Begins in Year / (4) Ends in Year / (5) Reserve					
Social Security $					
Retirement benefits					
Disability benefits					
Survivor's benefits					
Pension plans					
Employer					
Voluntary (IRA, Roth, 401[k], Keogh)					
Veteran's benefits					
Interest					
Dividends					
Early retirement bonus					
Insurance payments					
Life insurance					
Health insurance					
Long-term care insurance					
Disability insurance					
Conversion of personal investments					
Retirement savings					
General savings					
Property and goods					
Mutual funds					
Treasury bills					
Stocks					
Bonds					
Certificates					
Annuities					
Loans receivable					
Inheritances					
After-death inheritance					
Living inheritance (cash gift transfers)					

INCOME (2)	(1)	(2)	(3)	(4)	(5)
(1) Annual / (2) Monthly / (3) Begins in Year / (4) Ends in Year / (5) Reserve					
Working Income $					
Full-time employment:					
Part-time job:					
Part-time job:					
Self-employment income					
Residual income (royalties)					
In-kind income (companion, house tender)					
Home income					
Rental income					
Sale income					
Reverse mortgage					
Rental / sale of other real estate					
Gift income					
Personal holdings					
Sale of personal possessions					
Sale of collectibles					
Sale of car, boat, trailer, camper, etc.					
Other sales					
Use of emergency fund					
TOTAL INCOME $					

If this is a library book, please do not fill in this page! For a free, full-page download of this form, see www.super-second-life.com/form7A.htm

Second Life Expense Worksheet / Year or Age:					
EXPENSES	(1)	(2)	(3)	(4)	(5)
(1) Annual / (2) Monthly / (3) Begins in Year / (4) Ends in Year / (5) Reserve					
House payment or rent $					
Maintenance					
Furnishing					
Improvements					
Property tax					
Food					
Utilities					
Water					
Electricity					
Gas					
Oil					
Trash / Sewage					
Other:					
Inflation (2-3% a year)					
Phone					
Computer costs					
Clothing					
Purchases					
Cleaning					
Health costs					
Care					
Medicine					
Taxes					
Federal					
State					
Local					
Self-employment					
Transportation					
Car payments					
Gas, oil, repairs					
Parking					
Commuting / public transportation					

EXPENSES (2)	(1)	(2)	(3)	(4)	(5)
(1) Annual / (2) Monthly / (3) Begins in Year / (4) Ends in Year / (5) Reserve					
Professional fees $					
Gifts and donations					
Loan repayments					
Loan debts					
Personal care					
Care of family members or dependents					
Education					
Exercise / Fitness					
Travel / Vacation					
Savings investment					
Emergency fund					
Hobby costs					
Pets					
Entertainment					
Divorce costs (alimony, child support)					
Interest: credit card and other					
Assumed debts: children/others					
Insurance: Health					
Auto					
Property					
Life					
Disability					
Liability					
TOTAL EXPENSES $					

If this is a library book, please do not fill in this page! For a free, full-page download of this form, see www.super-second-life.com/form7B.htm

Second Life Money Worksheet / Year or Age:			
Annual basic living expenses		(A)	$
Annual basic income:			
Annual Social Security income	$		
Annual pension income	$		
Other annual income: Royalties	$		
Other annual income:	$		
Other annual income:	$		
Total income (add totals above)		(B)	$
Annual basic income deficit/surplus	(A) - (B)	(C)	$
Monthly supplemental income needed	÷12	$	
Special second life expenses this year	(from Action Plan)	(D)	$
Total money desired for this year	(A) + (D)	$	
Maximum income deficit/surplus	if C is -, (C) + (D) if C is +, (C) - (D)	(E)	$
Monthly supplemental income needed	÷12	$	
Additional income source(s):	Amount		
Income source:	$		
Income source:	$		
Income source:	$		
Income source:	$		
Income source:	$		
Income source:	$		
Income source:	$		
Income source:	$		
Additional income available this year	$	(F)	
Total income deficit/surplus this year	C + F	$	

Second Life Net Worth Worksheet / Year or Age:

NET WORTH	Now	1 Year	5	10	15
ASSETS					
Checking account(s) $					
Savings account(s)					
Bond(s)					
Certificate(s)					
Market value: home/apartment					
Market value: other real estate					
IRA and Keogh plans					
Cash value of life insurance					
Surrender value of annuities					
Equity: profit-sharing / pension					
Market value of stocks					
Market value of bonds					
Market value of mutual funds					
Current value of car(s)					
Current value of household furnishings and appliances					
Current value: furs and jewelry					
Loans receivable					
Other assets					
Total Assets (A) $					
LIABILITIES					
Mortgage balance $					
Loans: auto					
Loans: student					
Loans: home equity					
Current bills					
Credit-card balance					
Other debts:					
Total Liabilities (B) $					
Current Net Worth (A)-(B) $					

If this is a library book, please do not fill in this page! For a free, full-page download of this form, see www.super-second-life.com/form7D.htm

SECOND LIFE DREAM LIST

NAME _____ Date _____

DREAMS
1.
2.
3.
4.
5.
6.
7.
8.
9.
10.
11.
12.
13.
14.
15.
16.
17.
18.
19.
20.

TIME BOX

55-60:	60-65:
65-70:	70-75:
75-80:	80+:

If this is a library book, please do not fill in this page! For a free, full-page download of this form, see www.super-second-life.com/form9.htm

OUR FUTURE LIFE PLAN

SHARED DREAMS / Date:

_____ DREAMS	_____ DREAMS

CONFLICT RESOLUTION SHEET / Date:		
"What I want..."	"The Gap of Resolution"	"What I have..."

If this is a library book, please do not fill in this page! For a free, full-page download of this form, see www.super-second-life.com/form11.htm

ACTION PLAN	Date:
Dream:	**$**

ACTION STEPS

FINANCIAL CALCULATIONS	COSTS	POTENTIAL INCOME
	$	$
TOTALS	$	$

HEALTH CONSIDERATIONS

NOTES

Second Life Plan Time Line

	Both	
2005		
2010		
2015		
2020		
2025		
2030		

If this is a library book, please do not fill in this page! For a free, full-page download of this form, see www.super-second-life.com/form14A.htm

SECOND LIFE PROCESS CHECK-OFF CHART

Chapter / Item		Explanation	✓
2	"Me Now" List 1	The five lists help us see what we've	
2	"Me Now" List 2	done and learned, who we are now, and	
2	"Me Now" List 3	what we want to do later. A quick look	
2	"Me Now" List 4	at ourselves. They help pave the way to	
2	"Me Now" List 5	creating a more comprehensive and realistic Dream List.	
4	Second Life "In" List	What do we want to keep and/or build from in our later days?	
4	Second Life "Out" List	What do we want excluded from those later days?	
7	Second Life Income Worksheet	What we earn and gather now, and how we can change this when we wish in the future.	
7	Second Life Expense Worksheet	Where our money goes now, and may in the future. Shows where we can better economize when needed.	
7	Second Life Money Worksheet	The critical summary sheet. Can be updated at any point in the future. Needed for the Action Plan.	
7	Second Life Net Worth Worksheet	Shows what we are worth now and may be at key points in our future. Hard to plan not knowing this.	
8	Second Life Dream List	Without dreams, or direction, it's hard to plan a vital, fun, worthwhile future. The Action Plans start here.	
9	Time Box	Matches dreams to rough age categories, so we can best use our ability, energy, and wherewithal to make our dreams happen at the most appropriate time.	
10	Our Future Life Plan	Helps get in sync with your mate, to determine if the dream is yours, theirs, or shared.	

11	Conflict Resolu-tion Sheet	If needed, helps you resolve conflicts or get in gear and moving!	
12	Action Plan	One per dream, these are the core of creating our own Great Second Lives. They include the dream, cost, action steps, financial calculations, health considerations, and preparatory actions.	
13	Second Life Plan Time Line	Tells what we (and our mate) want to do when.	

If this is a library book, please do not fill in this page! For a free, full-page download of this form, see www.super-second-life.com/form14B.htm

GORDON BURGETT

◆ Gordon Burgett wrote the first edition of this book in 1999. He currently offers keynotes, workshops, and breakout sessions nationwide about this topic. (See *www.super-second-life.com.*)

◆ Since 1981, Burgett has also published 1,700+ articles and offered an average of 100 seminars and speeches annually. He has appeared extensively on radio and TV, as a guest author and a publishing specialist. Burgett is a long-standing member of the National Speakers Association, the American Society of Authors and Journalists, and the Publishers Marketing Association; has produced 26 audio cassette series and singles, and has published 25 books, including *Sell and Resell Your Magazine Articles; The Travel Writer's Guide; Standard Marketing Procedures for Dentists* (with Reece Franklin*); Publishing to Niche Markets; Treasure and Scavenger Hunts; Life After Dentistry* (with Dr. Jay Hislop)*; Niche Marketing for Writers, Speakers, and Entrepreneurs; Self-Publishing to Tightly-Targeted Markets; How to Sell More Than 75% of Your Freelance Writing; The Writer's Guide to Query and Cover Letters; Empire-Building by Writing and Speaking; Speaking for Money* (with Mike Frank)*; Ten Sales from One Article Idea,* and *The Query Book.* (See *www.gordonburgett.com.*)

◆ Four of Burgett's books have been Writer's Digest Book Club top choices*: Sell and Resell Your Magazine Articles, The Travel Writer's Guide, The Writer's Guide to Query and Cover Letters,* and *How to Sell More Than 75% of Your Freelance Writing.*

◆ Gordon has owned and directed a publishing company, Communication Unlimited, since 1981. It specializes in books, reports, and cassettes about writing, empire-building, and niche publishing. In 1995, the company expanded into Dental Communication Unlimited and Medical Communication Unlimited (see *www.sops.com.*). Recently his firm began a new imprint for academic administrators called Education Communication Unlimited (see *www.superintendents-and-principals.com*).

◆ Burgett earned four academic degrees: B.A., University of Illinois, Champaign-Urbana; M.A., University of Wisconsin, Madison; M.F.T. Thunderbird Graduate School, and M.A., Northern Illinois University . He was twice an university dean, taught Portuguese and history, created a city recreation program in Illinois, directed CARE (and Peace Corps) programs in Colombia and Ecuador (including the Land Directorship of the HOPE ship medical/dental program in Guayaquil), twice studied in Brazil, played professional baseball, led a gold hunt up the Paushi Yaco (Upper Amazon) River in Ecuador, and created Agemasters.

INDEX

Other Burgett Products

(All products are shipped the day the order is received.)

#	Title	Price	More information
	How to Plan a Great Second Life	$ 17.95	http://www.super-second-world.com/
	Treasure and Scavenger Hunts (B)	17.95	(B) Book
	How to Sell and Resell Your Magazine Articles (B)	17.95	(R) Report
	Travel Writer's Guide (B)	17.95	(A) Audio cassette
	60 Best U.S. Newspaper Travel Markets (R)	12.00	
	Empire-Building by Writing and Speaking (B)	12.95	Most products listed here are also available in digital download format, at a reduced price (and without shipping or tax.)
	Niche Marketing (B)	14.95	
	Publishing to Niche Markets (B)	14.95	
	How to Sell 75% of Your Travel Writing (A)	29.95	
	How to Publish Your Own Book and Earn $50,000 Profit! (A)	29.95	
	How to Set Up and Market Your Own Seminar (A)	44.95	Please see www. gordonburgett. com for each item.
	Writing Comedy Greeting Cards That Sell! (A)	29.95	
	Producing and Selling Your Own Audio Cassettes (A)	9.95	
	25 Professional Query and Cover Letters (R)	12.00	
	Speakers: How to Earn Happily Everafter with One Speech (R)	9.95	
	Using Your Book to Penetrate Your Niche Market (A)	9.95	
	Lian McAndrews and the Perfect Human World (B)	14.95	www.perfecthumanworld.com

Order Form

Please send this order by

FAX	(805) 937-3035. *Include this form please.*
E-MAIL	order@super-second-life.com
PHONE	(800) 563-1454 toll free. *Credit card ready?*
MAIL	P.O. Box 6405, Santa Maria, CA 93456.

Please put an X (or the quantity) before the item on the Product sheet.

I understand that I may return any item within 30 days for a full refund (less shipping)—for any reason, no questions asked.

[   ] Please send more information about Gordon Burgett speaking to our group or organization.
      Name of organization: _____

Name _____

Address _____

City _____ State _____ ZIP _____

Telephone _____ E-mail _____

Sales tax: Please add 7.75% for California orders.

Shipping: U.S. Please add $5 for first book or disk, $2 for each additional. We ship PRIORITY MAIL. For international orders or to ship media mail, please ask about the shipping costs by e-mail.

Payment: [   ] Check   [   ] VISA   [   ] Mastercard

Card number: _____

Expires _____ Name on card _____

(Please copy both the marked Product sheet and this, completed Order Form and submit them each time you order.)